Managing Cultural Joint Ventures

This book provides an in-depth exploration of two key aspects of managing cultural collaborations: managing the multiple identities of venture participants and managing the diverse images and brand relationships.

There is a variety of books available on mergers and acquisitions in the corporate world, but cultural joint ventures have not been examined in detail, and there are significant differences to consider. Cultural joint ventures are emerging as an important organisational structure in the creative sector. This is largely due to uncertainties in public funding, increased competition for audiences, and the ongoing search for innovative programming. Although arts organisations need to understand and manage these economic aspects, other aspects including internal culture, identity, and brand image are vital to the successful management of cultural joint ventures. Taking a global view and covering a variety of creative collaborations, the authors present case studies from Scandinavia, Europe, North and South America, and New Zealand.

From a managerial point of view, this book is valuable not only for a range of managers working in different types of cultural centres but also for managers working within various collaborative efforts in the creative industries more broadly. This will also be a valuable resource for researchers and scholars in the fields of arts management and marketing.

Tanja Johansson, PhD, is Director at the Laurea University of Applied Sciences in Espoo, Finland.

Annukka Jyrämä, PhD, is Professor of Cultural Management at the Estonian Academy of Music and Theatre and a senior advisor at Aalto University, Finland.

Kaari Kiitsak-Prikk, PhD, is Lecturer and Head of Studies on the Cultural Management MA programme at the Estonian Academy of Music and Theatre.

Routledge Research in the Creative and Cultural Industries
Series Editor: Ruth Rentschler

This series brings together book-length original research in cultural and creative industries from a range of perspectives. Charting developments in contemporary cultural and creative industries thinking around the world, the series aims to shape the research agenda to reflect the expanding significance of the creative sector in a globalised world.

Music as Labour
Inequalities and Activism in the Past and Present
Edited by Dagmar Abfalter and Rosa Reitsamer

Risk in the Film Business
Known Unknowns
Michael Franklin

Orchestra Management
Models and Repertoires for the Symphony Orchestra
Arne Herman

The Venice Arsenal
Between History, Heritage, and Re-use
Edited by Luca Zan

Managing Cultural Joint Ventures
An Identity-Image View
Tanja Johansson, Annukka Jyrämä and Kaari Kiitsak-Prikk

Public Relations as a Creative Industry
Elisenda Estanyol

For more information about this series, please visit: www.routledge.com/Routledge-Research-in-the-Creative-and-Cultural-Industries/book-series/RRCCI

Managing Cultural Joint Ventures

An Identity-Image View

Tanja Johansson, Annukka Jyrämä and Kaari Kiitsak-Prikk

Routledge
Taylor & Francis Group
LONDON AND NEW YORK

First published 2023
by Routledge
4 Park Square, Milton Park, Abingdon, Oxon OX14 4RN

and by Routledge
605 Third Avenue, New York, NY 10158

Routledge is an imprint of the Taylor & Francis Group, an informa business

British Library Cataloguing-in-Publication Data
A catalogue record for this book is available from the British Library

Library of Congress Cataloging-in-Publication Data
A catalog record has been requested for this book

ISBN: 978-0-367-22226-0 (hbk)
ISBN: 978-1-032-37475-8 (pbk)
ISBN: 978-0-429-27391-9 (ebk)

DOI: 10.4324/9780429273919

Typeset in Times New Roman
by Apex CoVantage, LLC

Table of contents

Figures

Tables

About the authors

Tanja Johansson, PhD, is working as Director at the Laurea University of Applied Sciences in Espoo, Finland. Previously she has worked as Vice Dean, Professor and Lecturer at the Sibelius Academy of the University of the Arts Helsinki, where she acted also as Head of Arts Management at the Sibelius Academy. Her research interests center on cultural joint ventures, regional impacts of arts, organisational identity, leadership, and organisational ethnography. Johansson has published in different academic journals such as International Journal of Arts Management, Creativity and Innovation Management, Event Management, and Journal of Arts Management, Law and Society, among others. She has also acted as the editor in chief of the European Journal of Cultural Management and Policy.

Annukka Jyrämä, PhD, is currently working as a professor at Estonian Academy of Music and Theatre in the Cultural Management programme and as a senior advisor in Aalto University. She is a docent on arts marketing and entrepreneurship at the Aalto University School of Business and at the Sibelius Academy of the University of the Arts Helsinki, Finland. Her research interests include branding, social responsibility, knowledge creation processes and the role of mediators from institutional and network theory perspectives. She holds the positions of trust in the Advisory board of the Foundation for Cultural Policy Research, Creative Finland and Network for Urban Studies. Her research articles have been published in several journals such as the International Journal of Arts Management, Marketing Intelligence and Planning, and Management Learning.

Kaari Kiitsak-Prikk, PhD, is a lecturer and head of studies at cultural management MA programme at the Estonian Academy of Music and Theatre. She has more than 15 years of experience working for the cultural management higher education in Estonia: managing international projects for curricula development, life-long learning training, publications, events, etc. She has been teaching subjects such as project management, career planning in the arts, cultural legislation, creative entrepreneurship, and leadership. Her research focuses on the public cultural sector; institutional setting of cultural management; cultural policy and governance; societal impact of arts; and societal engagement of HEIs. Also, she is interested in the research and practice of entrepreneurial training in higher arts education, career planning, mentorship, and professional coaching in the cultural sector.

Acknowledgements

We are extremely thankful for all the respondents of this longitudinal study on various cultural joint ventures. We have been involved in several cases in different countries and want to give our sincere gratitude for these arts and cultural organisations that make art happen night after night. During the years we have particularly interviewed executive and marketing managers, most of whom already worked for other organisations, and without your kind responses this study would not have been possible.

We also want to thank funders and supporters of this study: Wihuri Foundation, Finnish Foundation for Economic Education, HSE Support Foundation, Aalto University School of Business, Sibelius Academy of the University of the Arts Helsinki, and Estonian Academy of Music and Theatre. This support has been crucial for the execution and dissemination of this study.

1 Introduction

In recent years, collaboration, cooperation, interaction, participation, partnerships, and joint efforts have been emphasised in different contexts. We might even talk about a collaborative era in which different types of joint efforts, partnerships, and alliances have come to the forefront in order to create new opportunities and find synergies for new and exciting outcomes, as well as increased productivity. Studies on mergers and acquisitions, strategic alliances, and joint ventures have grown extensively, and different views have been adopted to understand the benefits and consequences of interorganisational efforts. Interestingly, even if different types of collaborative and joint efforts have taken place in the arts and cultural field for a long time, few studies have focused on this specific context.

Even if the cultural field has been characterised by various independent organisations, such as theatres, museums, and orchestras, different arts and cultural centres have had and still have an important role in serving artistic, cultural, social, economic, and urban objectives, both locally and internationally. Performing arts centres, museum districts, concert halls, dance centres, and cultural centres often involve two or more different arts organisations that share, for instance, facilities, marketing, restaurant services, and gift and other shops in order to benefit from the synergy of a common location in the same building or geographical area. We will define a cultural joint venture in more detail later in the chapter, but we begin here by describing the organisational and image-related view of arts and cultural organisations to paint a picture of the characteristics of these organisations and the reasons they cooperate.

1.1. The collaborative and cooperative era of arts and culture—a potential challenge and opportunity for management

The collaborative view of art-making and cultural production has a long history, which, instead of highlighting the individual creators, considers the

DOI: 10.4324/9780429273919-1

social and contextual (e.g., economic, social, and environmental) aspects that frame cultural productions and the networks involved. The focus is on the interaction between the artistic products, the producers (e.g., artistic, technical, and administrative participants involved in the processes through which artistic pieces are produced), and the audiences (e.g., customers and the public in general, critics and the media in general, and the other stakeholders that enable art to take place) (Becker, 1974, 1982; Bourdieu, 1993, 1992).

Becker (1974, 1982) calls the network of different actors an "art world," which can be seen as an "organized world of artistic activity, which constrains the range of choices and provides motives for making one or another of them" (Becker, 2006, p. 26). Becker (1982) argues for the sociological approach to art by describing that all the actors in a network are crucial to the creation of a cultural product. Artists are involved in the network in the same way as any others, and they are dependent on the cooperative links that provide a frame for the possibilities and opportunities of different outcomes. The art world described by Becker has become increasingly international and culturally diverse, the actors in the network are increasingly interdependent of each other, and this network has expanded to other fields to answer the demands of digitalisation, among other things.

Work in the field of cultural production is often organised in temporally limited projects and productions (e.g., Goodman & Goodman, 1976; Lindgren & Packendorff, 2007). The reasons for organising cultural productions in projects derive from the characteristics of the tasks involved; the projects or productions are often complex, unique, significantly important to the organisation, and defined in terms of the specific goals to be achieved within a certain time frame (Goodman & Goodman, 1976). The project-based work of cultural productions requires sensitivity to the desire, visions, improvisations (Lindqvist, 2007), and mutual trust of the production participants (Luonila, 2016), as well as the skilful engagement of various resources, not only mechanically but also aesthetically (Johansson, 2008). Furthermore, what characterises the work in these projects are the loyalty and professionalism, high ambition, responsibility, and dedication of the different participants (Lindgren & Packendorff, 2007). In addition, the level of ambiguity is usually high because the goals, schedules, funding, and team members might change on short notice. On the other hand, strong emotional involvement (e.g., Sauer, 2005) and intrinsic motivation (e.g., Eikhof & Haunschild, 2007) are also present, which make the participants willing to engage in one project or production after another.

Collective practices and collective expertise are also highlighted in many studies on cultural production. Collective expertise refers to work practices in which knowledge is constructed, shared, monitored, and connected through a collective of people (Koivunen, 2009; Parviainen, 2006; see also Lehtinen, 2022). Marotto et al. (2007) argue that individual virtuosity becomes collective in a group through a reflexive process in which the participants are transformed by their personal peak performance. This "collective virtuosity" refers to aesthetic experience on the collective level, a certain state of flow in which the sense of time is lost. In collective virtuosity, the participants interact with one another on cognitive, social, and aesthetic levels, leading to a group knowledge that is more than the sum of the participants' individual knowledge. Understanding the collaborative work in the arts and cultural field is central, not only on the individual level but also on the organisational level, as arts and cultural organisations increasingly collaborate with several other organisations and are involved in various networks in their respective fields (see e.g., Luonila, 2016; Luonila & Jyrämä, 2020).

A key aspect in arts and cultural productions is how to combine ambiguity and dynamism in practices that are challenged by unpredictable demand and ill-defined production processes (Lampel et al., 2000). On the demand side, cultural organisations seek to shape audience preferences by applying new methods of distribution, marketing, and promotion, and on the supply side, they aim to develop new ways of managing creative resources. In other words, a main managerial challenge of cultural organisations is finding a balance between creative and commercial values.

Researchers of issues related to management and organisations became interested in examining the various internal mechanisms of cultural and creative organisations, including organisational culture (e.g., Voss et al., 2000), organisational resources (e.g., Järvinen, 2019; Johansson, 2008), leadership (e.g., Koivunen, 2003; Lehtinen, 2022; Sauer, 2005), strategy (e.g., Maitlis & Lawrence, 2003), professional identity (e.g., Glynn, 2000), interorganisational relations (e.g., Atkinson, 2006; Maitlis, 2005), networks (e.g., Jyrämä, 2002; Jyrämä & Äyväri, 2010; Luonila, 2016), and institutional conditions (e.g., Agid & Tarondeau, 2007; Auvinen, 2000; Järvinen, 2019; Jyrämä & Äyväri, 2010). The following table summarises some of the characteristics of cultural organisations in order to understand this specific context of cultural joint ventures.

Table 1.1 Some characteristics of cultural organisations

	Characterising aspects	*Selected references*
Organisational values	Intrinsic value of artistic creativity, imagination, and autonomy often emphasised Prosocial values considered (e.g., community access, engagement, and involvement)	Voss et al. (2000)

(*Continued*)

Table 1.1 (Continued)

	Characterising aspects	*Selected references*
Structural characteristics	Structural differentiation of professionals depends on the size of the organisation Relatively low number of administrative staff Project- and production-based work combined with more formal organisational elements	Auvinen (2000); DiMaggio and Hirsch (1976)
Strategic decision-making	Diffuse power between artistic and administrative management Relatively low number of middle managers Selection of board members often connected to political orientation	DiMaggio (1987); Glynn (2000); Maitlis (2005); Maitlis and Lawrence (2003)
Brand image	Builds on identity, is aimed to differentiate and build understanding for the customer as to what the service or product entails Often uses key actors' (conductor, main performer, artist) names as identifiers Cultural field is often characterised by loyal customers	Aaker (1996); Jyrämä et al. (2015); Keller and Lehmann (2006)
Financial characteristics	Labour-intensive work Challenge of cost disease Unpredictable demand Government involvement in finances Difficulty of measuring success and quality of intangible products and services	Baumol and Bowen (1966); Lampel et al. (2000)
Leadership	Challenges of building trust between artistic and administrative personnel Strong emotional involvement of organisational members Aesthetic leadership practices highlighted (e.g., need for an auditive leadership culture)	Koivunen (2003, 2007); Lehtinen (2022); Reid and Karambayya (2009); Sauer (2005)
Relation to environment	Accountable for different instances, such as the arts field, funders, sponsors, and public in general Involvement of volunteers Political interventions possible Open to public scrutiny and review	DiMaggio and Powell (1983); Järvinen (2019); Luonila (2016)

Source: Adapted from Vilén (2010).

Next, we move on to discuss what we mean by cultural joint ventures and why we want to take, in particular, an identity-image view of these ventures.

1.2. What are cultural joint ventures and why do they matter?

Joint ventures are emerging as an important organisational structure in the cultural and creative sector. This is largely due to uncertainties in public funding, increased competition in outreach to audiences, and the ongoing search for new artistic content and innovative programming through collaboration. These structural and economic aspects are critical to understand and manage; however, issues of internal culture, identity, and brand image must also be considered in the successful management of cultural joint ventures (Clark et al., 2010; Gioia et al., 2010). Recently, we have witnessed new forms of joint venturing in the arts (Johansson & Jyrämä, 2016).

In some cultural joint ventures, no formal mergers or acquisitions have taken place; rather, they are essentially strategic alliances, defined as purposive relationships between two or more independent organisations that involve the exchange, sharing, or co-development of resources or capabilities to achieve mutually relevant benefits (Gulati, 1995, 1998). In some cases, joint ventures in the arts can be characterised as loosely coupled systems in which the actors are responsive to each other, but the systems remain separate with distinct identities (Orton & Weick, 1990; Weick, 1976). Regardless of their organisational form, however, joint ventures have a significant impact on organisational identity as well as brand identity and image (Jyrämä et al., 2015).

Dewey Lambert and Williams (2017) categorise the performing arts organisations into three types:

1) Producing companies that fund and create their own artistic works by employing their own artistic, administrative, and technical personnel
2) Presenting companies that acquire "ready-made" productions and sell them to audiences
3) Hosting companies that provide opportunities for other companies to rent their venues and facilities

In relation to the categorisation above, we will focus on cultural centres that have an element of the hosting company but often also either one or both other types of companies. By the term "cultural joint ventures," we want to emphasise the multiple roles different partnering organisations might have and the interorganisational collaboration that is involved in cultural venturing. With this view, we are also interested in examining the different phases partnering organisations often go through, which means that the roles and objectives of the partnering organisation and the hosting organisation might change due to different internal or external reasons. Therefore, we have selected to study cultural joint ventures in different phases, some at the very beginning and others with years or even decades of partnering with other organisations.

In the book, we present a number of cases we have been following over the last ten years. Thus, we have seen how different cultural joint ventures evolve over time, but it is good to bear in mind that the case descriptions provided often focus on a certain point of time in the journeys of different cultural joint ventures. We conducted semi-structured interviews with 27 people, starting in 2010, and it is natural that the key position holders, for instance, in general management and marketing, have changed over the years. Hence, the case descriptions might not represent the most recent situation in these organisations, but as a whole, they provide an interesting view of the different types and different maturities of cultural joint ventures around the world.

We argue that joint ventures in general and cultural joint ventures in particular will matter even more in the future. As discussed earlier, different types of collaboration and cooperation between organisations will continue to grow, and understanding these interorganisational opportunities and potential challenges at the managerial level is crucial. The lengthy COVID-19 pandemic has also forced arts organisations to find new ways of organising and branding. In the future, we might see even more international cultural joint ventures as digital opportunities are created among arts and cultural organisations.

1.3. Identity-image view of managing cultural joint ventures

During our longitudinal study on cultural joint ventures, we have been interested in understanding their identity and branding processes. The reasons for this particular focus are multiple:

- We are interested in the evolvement of the interorganisational processes, and an identity-image view provides both an internal and external view of the cultural joint ventures
- We are interested in expanding the existing views of organisational identities, images, and branding by focusing on the interorganisational level of these processes
- We believe that the identity-image view provides an opportunity to take into account the organisational and interorganisational values that create a crucial basis for the leadership of arts organisations and the collaboration among them

This book will provide knowledge about the effects that joint-venture structures might have on organisational identity and branding. Our aim is also to provide insights for cultural centre executives involved in managing their staff and organisations towards cultivating strong brands and brand alliances. In practice, cultural joint ventures refer, for instance, to cultural centres that host several artistic organisations, such as symphony orchestras, opera companies, theatre groups, and other artistic groups. Often, these cultural joint ventures involve a separate administrative entity to manage the joint practices. There seems to be only a small number of studies written about joint ventures in the public sector in general and the cultural sector in particular, apart from studies on industry-level networks (see Sedita, 2008). From a managerial point of view, this book is valuable not only for a range of managers working in different types of cultural centres but also for managers working within various collaborative efforts in the creative industries more broadly.

1.4. Objectives of the book

The primary objective of the book is to provide a comprehensive identity-image view of managing cultural joint ventures. There are a variety of books available on mergers and acquisitions in the corporate world, but cultural joint ventures have not been examined in detail, and there are significant differences to consider. For example, ownership within a cultural joint venture is often a complex combination of public organisations and their affiliates, leading to a multidimensional network of identities that needs to be managed. In addition, cultural joint ventures in the arts and other creative fields have not been considered from the identity-image point of view.

Another important objective of the book is to provide international perspectives on managing cultural joint ventures by drawing from multiple cases from different continents. The authors have studied international cases for several years and will present a valuable collection. The proposed book focuses on the following themes:

- Managing multiple organisational identities and diverse cultures in cultural joint ventures
- Managing multiple brand images and diverse brand relationships involved in cultural joint ventures
- Bridging the identity-image view of cultural joint ventures to allow coherence in managing these ventures
- Highlighting the connectedness of organisational identity, brand identity, and brand image through global examples and case studies, and making recommendations for navigating challenging joint-venture situations

1.5. Structure of the book

The book starts with an introduction, which provides definitions and a historical background, reviews current research on the topic, states the objectives of the book, and describes the structure of the book. The introduction provides the reader with an overview of the key elements from current academic discussions about organisational identity, brand identity, and image, and offers insights into their connectedness, with multiple examples from professional and academic sources. The discussion focuses on the challenges faced in joint ventures in creative and artistic settings. In the introduction, the key concepts are explained, with arguments provided as to why each topic requires a deeper look. In addition, the introduction provides explanations of the main challenges faced by managers of cultural joint ventures, focusing on issues of organisational identity, brand identity, and image. The structure and goals of the book are provided to guide the reader through the various parts.

Following the introduction, there are three main chapters: managing identities, managing images, and bridging the two views. These chapters include introductions to the topics presented, a theoretical framing of the topics, and practical examples of international cultural joint ventures. Each chapter includes three to four sub-chapters. A large number of cases illustrates topics throughout the book, providing a path for the reader to integrate the connectedness and insights from each section of the book. In each section, additional examples are given to highlight a particular topic or issue. The three main sections of the book are followed by two final chapters: a discussion of the future of cultural joint ventures and some final words.

The international cases explored in the book are Concertgebaum (Amsterdam, Netherlands), Copenhagen Concert Hall (Copenhagen, Denmark), Helsinki Music Centre (Helsinki, Finland), Auckland Live (Auckland, New Zealand), Harpa (Reykjavik, Iceland), Gran Theatre Nacional (Lima, Peru), Seattle Symphony, and Opera Players' Organization (Washington, United States). In the first part of the book, the cases are examined through the lenses of organisational identities in the context of cultural joint ventures. In the second part, the focus is on the image and brand identity, and the third part combines the views and presents a more holistic approach to managing cultural joint ventures. The case presentations involve specific managerial challenges and present certain managerial responses in relation to specific cases.

The fourth part of the book takes a more general view on managing cultural joint ventures and considers what these ventures might look like in the future. As the COVID-19 pandemic has affected the arts and cultural sector severely, we dedicate some part of the chapter to reviewing the consequences of the pandemic and explore the potential new openings for cultural joint ventures in the post-COVID world. In addition, we consider other environmental challenges that will force arts and cultural organisations to cooperate and join their activities in innovative and pathbreaking ways in the future. The book concludes with some closing remarks and presents avenues for further research within the cultural joint ventures.

References

Aaker, D. A. (1996). *Building strong brands*. New York: The Free Press.

Agid, P., & Tarondeau, J.-C. (2007). Governance of major cultural institutions: The case of Paris opera. *International Journal of Arts Management, 10*(1).

Atkinson, P. (2006). *Everyday arias. An operatic ethnography*. Lanham, MD: AltaMira Press.

Auvinen, T. (2000). *Unmanageable opera? The artistic-economic dichotomy and its manifestations in the organizational structures of five opera organizations*. Doctoral dissertation, London City University.

Baumol, W. J., & Bowen, W. G. (1966). *Performing arts: The economic dilemma*. New York: Twentieth Century Fund.

Becker, H. S. (1974). Art as collective action. *American Sociological Review, 39*(6), 767–776.

Becker, H. S. (1982). *Art worlds*. Berkeley, CA: University of California Press.

Becker, H. S. (2006). The work itself. In H. S. Becker, R. R. Faulkner, & B. Kirshenblatt-Gimblett (Eds.), *Art from start to finish: Jazz, painting, writing, and other improvisations*. Chicago, IL: The University of Chicago Press.

Bourdieu, P. (1992). *The rules of art. Genesis and structure of the literary field*. Stanford, CA: Stanford University Press.

Bourdieu, P. (1993). *The field of cultural production*. Oxford: Polity Press.

Clark, M., Gioia, D. A., Ketchen, D. J., Jr. & Thomas, J. B. (2010). Transitional identity as a facilitator of organizational identity change during a merger. *Administrative Science Quarterly*, *55*, 397.

Dewey Lambert, P., & Williams, R. (2017). The professionalization of performing arts center management. In P. Dewey Lambert & R. Williams (Eds.), *Performing arts center management*. London: Routledge.

DiMaggio, P. (1987). The production of culture in the music industry: The ASCAP-BMI controversy. *Administrative Science Quarterly, 32*(4), 607–609.

DiMaggio, P., & Hirsch, P. M. (1976). Production organizations in the arts. *American Behavioral Scientist, 19*(6), 735–753.

DiMaggio, P. J., & Powell, W. W. (1983). The iron cage revisited: Institutional isomorphism and collective rationality in organizational fields. *American Sociological Review*, *48*(2), 147–160.

Eikhof, D. R., & Haunschild, A. (2007). For art's sake! Artistic and economic logics in creative production. *Journal of Organizational Behavior, 28*(5), 523–538.

Gioia, D. A., Price, K. N., Hamilton, A. L., & Thomas, J. B. (2010). Forging an identity: An insider-outsider study of processes involved in the formation of organizational identity. *Administrative Science Quarterly*, *55*(1), 1–46.

Glynn, M. A. (2000). When cymbals become symbols: Conflict over organizational identity within a symphony orchestra. *Organization Science*, *11*(3), 285–298.
Goodman, R. A., & Goodman, L. P. (1976). Some management issues in temporary systems: A study of professional development and manpower—the theater case. *Administrative Science Quarterly*, *21*(3), 494–501.
Gulati, R. (1995). Social structure and alliance formation patterns: A longitudinal analysis. *Administrative Science Quarterly*, *40*(4), 619–652.
Gulati, R. (1998). Alliances and networks. *Strategic Management Journal*, *19*(4), 293–317.
Järvinen, T. (2019). *The challengers of public cultural centres. A mixed method study on private cultural centres in Finland*. Helsinki: Unigrafia.
Johansson, M. (2008). *Engaging resources for cultural events: A performative view*. Doctoral dissertation, Stockholm School of Economics.
Johansson, T., & Jyrämä, A. (2016). Network of organizational identities in the formation of a cultural joint venture: A case study of the Helsinki Music Centre. *International Journal of Arts Management*, *18*(3), 67–78.
Jyrämä, A. (2002). Contemporary art markets—structure and actors: A study of art galleries in Finland, Sweden, France, and Great Britain. *International Journal of Arts Management*, *4*(2), 50–65.
Jyrämä, A., & Äyväri, A. (2010). Marketing contemporary visual art. *Marketing Intelligence and Planning*, *28*(6), 723–735.
Jyrämä, A., Kajalo, S., Johansson, T., & Sirén, A. (2015). Arts organizations and branding: Creating a new joint brand for three arts organizations. *Journal of Law, Society and Arts Management*, *45*(3), 193–206.
Keller, K. L., & Lehmann, D. D. (2006). Brands and branding: Research findings and future priorities. *Marketing Science*, *25*(6), 740–759.
Koivunen, N. (2003). *Leadership in symphony orchestras: Discursive and aesthetic practices*. Tampere: Tampere University Press.
Koivunen, N. (2007). The processual nature of leadership discourses. *Scandinavian Journal of Management*, *23*(3), 285–305.
Koivunen, N. (2009). Collective expertise: Ways of organizing expert work in collective settings. *Journal of Management & Organization*, *15*(2), 258–276.
Lampel, J., Lant, T., & Shamsie, J. (2000). Balancing act: Learning from organizing practices in cultural industries. *Organization Science*, *11*(3), 263–269.
Lehtinen, V. K. (2022). *Emergent self-direction in an organization, case symphony orchestra: "Why does the orchestra play well, even if it is conducted poorly?"* Lappeenranta: LUT Yliopistopaino.
Lindgren, M., & Packendorff, J. (2007). Performing arts and the art of performing. On co-construction of project work and professional identities in theatres. *International Journal of Project Management*, *25*, 354–364.
Lindqvist, K. (2007). Eros and Apollo. The curator as pas-de-deux leader. In P. Guillet de Monthoux, C. Gustafsson, & S.-E. Sjöstrand (Eds.), *Aesthetic leadership: Managing fields of flow in art and business*. London: Palgrave Macmillan.
Luonila, M. (2016). *Festivaalituotannon merkitysten verkosto ja johtaminen. Tapaustutkimuksia suomalaisista taidefestivaaleista*. Helsinki: Unigrafia.

Luonila, M., & Jyrämä, A. (2020). Does co-production build on co-creation or does co-creation result in co-producing? *Arts and the Market*, *10*(1), 1–17.

Maitlis, S. (2005). The social processes of organizational sensemaking. *Academy of Management Journal*, *48*(1), 21–49.

Maitlis, S., & Lawrence, T. B. (2003). Orchestral manoeuvres in the dark: Understanding failure in organizational strategizing. *Journal of Management Studies*, *40*(1), 109–139.

Marotto, M., Roos, J., & Victor, B. (2007). Collective virtuosity in organizations: A study of peak performance in an orchestra. *Journal of Management Studies*, *44*(3), 388–413.

Orton, J. D., & Weick, K. E. (1990). Loosely coupled systems: A reconceptualization. *The Academy of Management Review*, *15*(2), 203–223.

Parviainen, J. (Ed.). (2006). *Kollektiivinen asiantuntijuus [Collective expertise]*. Tampere: Tampere University Press.

Reid, W., & Karambayya, R. (2009). Impact of dual executive leadership dynamics in creative organizations. *Human Relations*, *62*(7), 1073–1112.

Sauer, E. (2005). *Emotions in leadership: Leading a dramatic ensemble*. Tampere: Tampere University Press.

Sedita, S. R. (2008). Interpersonal and inter-organizational networks in the performing arts: The case of project-based organizations in the live music industry. *Industry and Innovation*, *15*(5), 493–511.

Vilén, T. (2010). *Being in between. An ethnographic study on opera and relational identity construction*. Helsinki: Edita.

Voss, G. B., Cable, D. M., & Voss, Z. G. (2000). Linking organizational values to relationships with external constituents: A study of nonprofit professional theatres. *Organization Science*, *11*(3), 330–347.

Weick, K. E. (1976). Educational organizations as loosely coupled systems. *Administrative Science Quarterly*, *21*, 1–19.

Part I

Managing the multiple identities of cultural joint ventures

Identities in organisations have been considered to be multiple, hybrid, in flux, and under negotiation for quite some time. The potential for multiple views of an organisation is also a theoretical starting point for this book, which contends that both individual and joint organisational efforts provide multiple opportunities for identity construction. Part I of the book introduces the organisational identity view by describing the multiple sources of organisational identities in cultural joint ventures and examining how multiple identities may affect organisational practices, particularly in complex organisational contexts. The first chapter of Part I focuses on the current understandings of organisational identities and how identities may shift and act in contradictory ways.

In many organisations, identities may be challenged by complex ownership ties, conflicting interests, and multifaceted expectations. All these challenges must be handled carefully for a mutually rewarding outcome. On the other hand, complex organisational contexts, such as in the case of cultural joint ventures, provide an exciting platform for developing new creative contents and building a strong sense of community if the identities are managed well. The chapters include a presentation of three cases that illuminate the challenges and opportunities of managing multiple organisational identities. These cases are employed throughout the book and considered from different perspectives. In addition, several short cases are presented in the chapter to highlight the managerial implications for the topics discussed in Part I.

DOI: 10.4324/9780429273919-2

2 Multiple organisational identities within cultural joint ventures

2.1. Different understandings of organisational identities

Identity is a widely used concept that has generated a range of studies across disciplines, such as the social sciences, psychology, and philosophy. Each discipline has traditionally put an emphasis on different approaches, which has contributed to a great variation in the terminology and level of analysis used. In general, identities, as well as organisational and management studies, have become a popular research topic that has contributed to exploring organisations and organisational life in many ways. Since the pathbreaking study on organisational identity by Stuart Albert and David A. Whetten in 1985, various philosophical, theoretical, and methodological approaches have been applied in the studies on this subject. The different approaches to the topic have moved between monolithic and multiple identities as well as between the essentialist and constructed approaches to identities (Alvesson et al., 2008; Pratt, 2018).

The majority of research on organisational identity is based on the view that identity is a relational concept in that it is constructed in interaction with others (e.g., Albert & Whetten, 1985; Ashforth & Mael, 1989; Dutton & Dukerich, 1991). In the organisational identity literature, it is a broadly accepted view that organisational identity can be considered as what is central, distinctive, and enduring about an organisation (Albert & Whetten, 1985). Albert and Whetten (1985) argued that organisational identity is formed by a process of ordered inter-organisational comparisons and reflections over time. Hence, organisational identity places the organisation in a social space by naming it as being like certain organisations and unlike others (e.g., Glynn & Abzug, 2002). Fiol et al. (1998) considered an organisation's identity to be an aspect of culturally embedded sensemaking that is organisationally self-focused, whereas Weick (1995) approached organisational identity as a collectively held frame within which organisational

DOI: 10.4324/9780429273919-3

participants make sense of their world. Hatch and Schultz (2002) emphasised contextuality and reflexivity in organisational identity dynamics, which refers to the process through which organisational members understand and explain themselves as an organisation. Organisational identity thus involves a shared understanding by a collective (Corley et al., 2006); it is a product of the dialectic relationship between collective, shared cognition on the one hand and socially structured individual cognition on the other (Haslam & Ellemers, 2005).

The traditional conception of organisational identity, in which the members distinguish their organisation from other organisations and adhere to these rather enduring beliefs, has been challenged by scholars who are more inclined to interpretive research. For instance, from an interpretive perspective, organisational identities can be seen in terms of intersubjective understandings created through negotiations of meanings among the organisational members (Clegg et al., 2007). Meanings refer here, in particular, to the values, beliefs, and/or feelings which are represented by artifacts beyond their literal references (see Yanow, 2003). Looking at organisational identities from this point of view means that organisational members may relate multiple meanings to their organisation, which may or may not be shared by the other members of the same organisation. This may also indicate that different variations of the shared meanings can exist simultaneously in organisations, but these variations may change over time (e.g., Golden-Biddle & Rao, 1997; Hatch & Schultz, 2002; Cloutier & Ravasi, 2020).

Therefore, depending on the situation, the members of an organisation may take a certain view on a particular issue and also express uncertainty or offer critique concerning other issues (Alvesson, 2003; Alvesson et al., 2008; Pratt, 2018). These so-called meaning-making processes in organisations are constantly shaped and impacted by the relations organisational members have with each other, with their organisation, and with the organisation's larger environment (e.g., Ybema et al., 2009). Interorganisational collaboration, which is at the core of this book, tends to put even more focus on what happens outside and between the different organisations. Meaning-making processes between different organisations have been studied in particular in the context of mergers and acquisitions (M&A) (see Tienari & Vaara, 2016), but studies in the context of joint ventures or strategic alliances, in which no formal M&A have taken place, have been less in focus.

The dynamic interplay between organisational members, through which organisational identities are negotiated, has also been examined through sensemaking and sense-giving processes. In these processes, organisational members "periodically reconstruct shared understandings and revise formal claims of what their organisation is and stands for" (Ravasi & Schultz, 2006, p. 436). Hence, the processes of identity construction can be seen to work in-between the forces that seek to define more durable identities and those that challenge current views (Clegg et al., 2007; Parker, 2007). Several studies also stress that in the process of changing or transforming identities, the internal organisational image (i.e., the organisation's own view of its identity) and the external organisational image (i.e., the way it is perceived by outside actors, such as customers or media) are equally important (e.g., Gioia & Thomas, 1996; Gioia et al., 2010; Hatch & Schultz, 2008; Ravasi & Schultz, 2006). Hatch and Schultz (1997, 2002) argue that organisational identity needs to be theorised in relation to both culture and image in order to understand how the internal and external definitions of organisational identity interact. This is also one of the grounding approaches of this book, and this interaction will be discussed more closely in Parts II and III.

Some key concepts within the field of organisational identity

There is a number of related concepts that are important to understand in relation to the concept of organisational identity, such as social identity, corporate identity, and organisational identification.

Social identity refers to individuals' knowledge that they belong to certain groups, together with the emotional and value significance of these group memberships. Hence, social identity tends to be seen as an internalised knowledge structure and has been studied through various processes, such as categorisation of self and others, the fluidity of identities and identifications, the contextual and negotiated aspects of multiple identities, and the conflicts between different identities (Cornelissen et al., 2007).

Corporate identity can be defined as a distinctive public image a corporate entity communicates that structures people's engagement with it. Corporate identity is thus seen as a projected image of an organisation and has often been studied through organisational material and artifacts (e.g., logos, slogans, or other aesthetic aspects), tangible contents, or perceptions of stakeholders (Cornelissen et al., 2007).

Organisational identification refers to the process(es) through which individuals come to attach their self-definition to their perceptions of the organisation (e.g., Ashforth & Mael, 1989; Dutton et al., 1994; Ravasi & Van Rekom, 2003), that is, the ways people draw on their membership in organisations in their constructions of self. Researchers concerned with organisational identification increasingly recognise, in principle, that it refers not just to a state but to multiple simultaneously occurring and interrelated dynamic processes, as people continuously reassess and revise their relationships with the organisations to which they belong (e.g., Ashforth et al., 2008; Atewologun et al., 2017; Cornelissen et al., 2007; Haslam, 2004; Hogg & Terry, 2000).

Organisational identity work refers to the various individual-level processes of identity construction in organisations (Brown, 2017), and it serves as an explanatory concept by offering an analytical tool to investigate the role of micro-processes in the production of macro-consequences (Brown, 2017).

Organisational identity metaphors refer to a figure of speech to suggest a resemblance between the characteristics of individuals and the characteristics of a collective (Cornelissen, 2002). Organisational identity as a metaphor has been useful in theorising how organisations are similar to and different from individuals and other collectives (Gioia et al., 2002), and in understanding the symbolic dimensions of organisational life (Cornelissen, 2002).

2.2 Between multiple and hybrid identities

In arts and cultural management studies, the theoretical lenses of organisational identities have been applied to study, for instance, symphony orchestras (Maitlis & Lawrence, 2003), game companies (Tuori & Vilén, 2011), opera houses (Beech et al., 2012; Vilén, 2010), and music centres (Johansson & Jyrämä, 2016). The theoretical views have been more on the constructive and discursive end of the dimension of paradigms, and more qualitative than quantitative approaches have been applied to these studies.

As discussed earlier, it is not a new phenomenon to consider identities as plural and organisations as having more than one identity. However, plurality may refer to various aspects, such as multiple categories for an organisation to draw from pluralistic institutional contexts or be influenced by multiple institutional logics. The plurality of identities may also be linked to a role an organisation has, what it does, and who it serves, or it can refer to different views of organisational groups who define their organisation differently (Pratt, 2018; see also Klein & Amis, 2018 for pluralistic organisational identities). According to Pratt (2018), at least two main streams of research within organisational identity plurality can be identified: 1) a stream that considers organisational identities to be *multiple* and 2) a stream that considers organisational identities to be *hybrid*.

Pratt (2018) states that multiple organisational identities may have different meanings depending on the different conceptualisations of the identities. This may refer to multiple categories, multiple roles or multiple groups in the organisation, and each of these views might have a different understanding of "who" the organisation is.

Hence, Pratt (2018) distinguishes three different ways of approaching multiple organisational identities:

- **Multiple organisational categories**
    - such as multiple institutional logics that an organisation relates to

- **Multiple organisational roles**
  - such as multiple conceptualisations of what an organisation does and for whom
- **Multiple organisational groupings**
  - such as different professional or other groups within an organisation who define their organisation differently

A theoretical example related to multiple organisational categories can be found in Onishi's (2019) study, in which he considers identity as an integral part of the mechanism by which logics shape organisational decision-making. His findings confirm identity's overall mediating effects and offer new insights into how nonprofit organisations in particular respond to logic-identity incompatibility. Onishi (2019) argues that social identity has a dominant role in consistently suppressing external pressures from commercial logic, whereas businesslike identity overcomes social-welfare logic only when associated with nonprofit status (Onishi, 2019).

The second stream, hybrid identities, refers to two organisational identities that, according to Albert and Whetten, "are not expected to go together" (1985, p. 270). The two identities are experienced as essential and unalterable but incompatible and at odds with each other. However, Albert and Whetten (1985) added that the two identities are not just either-or, but can vary along certain dimensions, such as the normative-utilitarian dimension. Utilitarian identities refer, for instance, to a "for-profit"-focused understanding of the organisation, whereas normative identities refer to a nonmonetary-focused understanding of identities. In arts organisations, the normative-utilitarian dimension is clearly present in their everyday life; utilitarian identities focus on the accountability, efficiency, and funding of the organisation, whereas normative identities emphasise artistic and aesthetic values, cultural heritage, and creativity.

2.3. Multiple and hybrid identities in arts and cultural organisations

In arts and cultural organisations, multiple and hybrid identities are constantly present for several reasons. First, the competing logics of art and economy, and increasingly also social logic, create tensions that provide multiple sources for identity construction (e.g., Vilén, 2010). Second, societal expectations are multiple, particularly for publicly funded organisations, and many arts and cultural organisations are expected to measure and show their social as well as societal impact (Anttonen et al., 2016; Noh &

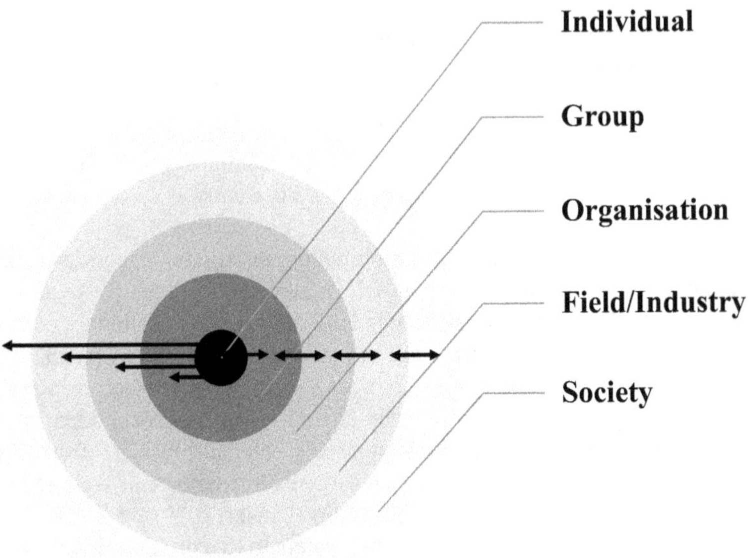

Figure 2.1 Multiple sources for identity construction through interrelated relations

Tolbert, 2019). Third, artists working in a cultural organisation may have several employers and a freelance career besides their work in the institution. Hence, some artists may experience competing work contexts due to differences in organisational- and field-level expectations (Vilén, 2010).

The following figure illustrates the multifaceted context of arts and cultural organisations with multiple interrelations between different actors at the individual, group, organisational, field (or industry), and societal levels. The interrelations may occur from level to level, but they may also take place directly, for example between an individual organisational member and society.

The multiple resources for organisational identity construction may appear at the different levels of individual, group (e.g., professional groups), organisation, field, and society as well as within the different interrelations of these. In arts organisations, in particular, individuals seem to draw from multiple sources and also directly from societal- and field-level sources. The ways cultural and creative organisations are interconnected to their field and the society through their organisational members and groups create many positive opportunities for organisations to develop and to be connected to their societal contexts. However, these multilayered interrelations may also create challenges for the management of these organisations, which is discussed next.

3 Managing interorganisational identities

3.1. Interrelated levels of identities

Different levels of analysis in the research on organisational identities have been conducted over the years, and the distinction between individual (personal) and collective (social) identities has been a common ground. There have also been attempts, however, to explore the intersubjective level of identities. For instance, Brewer and Gardner (1996) base identities on the notion that individuals tend to define themselves in terms of their engagement in relationships with others and with larger social groups. They distinguish between individual, interpersonal, and collective identities based on the personal, relational, and collective self-conceptions.

However, the distinction between individual and collective identities is inherently ambiguous because they are often blurred and overlapping in organisational practices (see Collinson, 2006). Sluss and Ashford (2007) argue that the research on organisational identities has usually focused either on the individual or the collective levels, while the interpersonal level in organisational context has received less attention. In line with Brewer and Gardner's (1996) categorisation, Sluss and Ashforth (2007) draw from the view that individuals are interdependent of each other and argue that organisational identities derive from interpersonal comparisons (individual-level identity), role-related relationships (interpersonal-level identity), and intergroup comparisons (collective-level identity). Sluss and Ashforth (2007) argue that the relational identity approach provides an integrative construct that can help to integrate the different levels of identities.

What has not often been considered in the previous categorisations is the *interorganisational* level of identity construction. The interorganisational level refers to the processes of identity construction between two or more organisations. In interorganisational identity construction, organisational members relate to organisations other than the one they belong to. In the case of joint ventures or other types of more informal joint efforts between

DOI: 10.4324/9780429273919-4

Table 3.1 Intergroup level of analysis

Level of analysis	*Self-concept*	*Basis of self-evaluation*	*Frame of reference*	*Basic social motivation*
Individual	Personal	Traits	Interpersonal comparison	Self-interest
Interpersonal	Relational	Roles	Reflection	Other's benefit
Group	Collective	Group prototype	Intergroup comparison	Collective welfare
Intergroup	Relational	Group roles	Intergroup reflection	Joint benefits

Source: Adapted from Brewer & Gardner (1996, p. 84).

organisations, interorganisational identity construction may involve comparing and contrasting between organisations, identifications or misidentifications between organisations, and multiple meaning-making processes between organisations (see e.g., Beech & Huxham, 2003).

In this book, we are particularly interested in the level of interorganisational identity construction and aim to make visible the relational processes involved in it. Nevertheless, the other levels of individual, interpersonal, and group organisation identities are present as well. We call these interrelated processes of identity construction a *net of identities* in which multiple sources of identity construction for questions such as "who am I" and "who are we" are present and available for the organisational members to make sense of (Johansson & Jyrämä, 2016).

3.2 Processes of interorganisational identity construction

While the complexity of organising has increased in the contemporary economy, the resources for organisational identity construction have become more diverse (e.g., Parker, 2007). Particularly, the increased complexity of organising is in our interest, as the situation of joint ventures and other types of strategic partnerships potentially challenge the earlier resources for identity construction. Continuous changes within and between organisations add also to the complexity of organising, particularly in mergers and acquisitions (Clark et al., 2010), corporate spin-offs (Corley & Gioia, 2004), forming of strategic alliances (Wohlstetter, Smith & Malloy, 2005) and the founding of a new unit as part of a larger organisation (Gioia et al., 2010). These rather radical changes may lead the organisational members to form new sources for identity construction and to transform their existing views of "who we are as an organisation."

Van Knippenberg (2016) considers the relationship between organisational change and organisational identity to be multifaceted. On the one hand, organisational identity may motivate resistance to change if the change is considered as a threat to the existing organisational identity. On the other hand, the existing organisational identity may help the organisational members to accept the change if the change is considered to safeguard the continuity of organisational identity. We have investigated organisational identity construction in the context of cultural joint venture formation in which the participating organisations are making sense of the ambiguity of existing organisational identities, the identities of the affiliated organisations (the owners of the participating organisations), and the identities of the new joint venture in the unusual setting in which there is no distinct organisation or unit that holds the power position over the others.

Within the cases studied in this book, we have identified several processes related to the interorganisational level of identity construction. These processes can be themed as four distinctive ways of constructing interorganisational identities:

1) **Protective**
2) **Hostile**
3) **Selective**
4) **Supportive**

First, we identified *protective* processes against the other organisations involved in the joint venture. This was concretised in the ways individual organisations strengthened their own identities, for instance in renewing their websites and brand images before participating in the joint venture. Second, there appeared to be *hostile* processes against all the other organisations or against a certain organisation partaking in the joint venture. This was seen in the ways and pace with which organisations were collaborating in the practical matters in their everyday life. Particularly the nonprofit and for-profit organisations within the same joint venture experienced hostile processes due to different value bases and different goals.

Thirdly, some of the processes of interorganisational identity construction were *selective*. This refers to the way certain organisations within the joint venture found a common ground for collaboration and joint activities, whereas others kept working on their own or with partners that they had had before the joint venture. The selective grouping of organisations in joint ventures can have both positive and negative consequences. For example, more intensive collaboration of two or more organisations working in the same artistic field (e.g., symphony orchestras) or within the same production type (e.g., festivals) refers to a positive selective process. On the other hand, negative selective processes may occur if groups of organisations within a cultural joint venture start to compete with each other, for instance about the same marketing and communication resources available for the joint venture.

Finally, there can be *supportive* processes in which the venturing organisations aim to build mutually beneficial activities. Supportive processes seemed to be more common in joint ventures representing the same art form but operating in different fields of it (e.g., a symphony orchestra and a choir). In addition, the phase and maturity of venturing seemed to affect the ways organisations acted supportively towards each other. In the beginning of the joint venture, the partnering organisations seemed to focus more on the protective and hostile sides, whereas later on, when the organisations got to know others' practices, they were able to focus more on supporting each other.

3.3 The role of leadership in interorganisational identity construction

An important question to be examined is also how leadership practices may affect the sensemaking processes of organisational and interorganisational identity construction. Van Knippenberg (2016) argues that organisational leaders are required to have both credibility and legitimacy in their attempts to influence and change organisational members' views of organisational identity. In Van Knippenberg's view, leader group prototypicality is a key to leaders' ability to influence organisational members' understanding of organisational identities.

In the context of joint ventures, the existing organisations might have a clear understanding of their present identity, but the interorganisational venture often has, in the beginning, a relatively undefined understanding of its identity. Consistent communication of the organisational identity to support strategic or other types of organisational change has been presented as one of the main tools for leaders to influence change in organisational identity. This sense-giving activity requires a deep understanding of the ways organisational members and leaders make sense of their organisation in order to forge linkages between the existing and envisioned understanding of the organisational identity (Gioia & Chittipeddi, 1991; Gioia et al., 2000; Van Knippenberg, 2016).

Another tool for leaders to change understandings of organisational identity is to draw from the history and the nostalgic past of the organisation. Longstanding arts and cultural organisations tell historic and even heroic stories of their past. What we will see in the following case studies is that there were difficulties in envisioning the identity of newly built joint ventures. For leaders, it is crucial to also "walk the identity talk" and act as role models for the envisioned future. In the newly built cultural joint ventures, the leaders of the organisations may also have inconsistent identity claims, which do not help to create a shared understanding of the joint venture. In the context of mergers and acquisitions, Tienari and Vaara (2016) argue that mergers tend to call for a heightened sense of belonging to a specific group and at the same time create a pressure to identify with new groups. In these situations, cultural belonging becomes increasingly important (Tienari & Vaara, 2016), and that might also be a way for leaders to help build new groundings for organisational identity construction.

Even if this book does not focus on mergers and acquisitions, there seem to be rather similar observations on belonging and identification in the cases in which two or more cultural organisations become joint ventures or strategic alliances of some sort.

Next, we will explore these interorganisational processes of identity construction in the cases of cultural joint ventures. We draw from various international cases that have been examined during the different phases of joint venturing.

4 Cases and managerial implications of cultural joint ventures

4.1. Case 1: Helsinki Music Centre, Helsinki, Finland

The Helsinki Music Centre (HMC) can be conceptualised as a joint venture without any formal merger or acquisition taking place. Helsinki Music Centre is located in the capital city of Finland. The Centre was opened in 2011 after 20 years of planning and negotiating the finances and ownerships, organising an architecture competition for the building, constructing the world-class music centre, and finally planning for the everyday practices and division of responsibilities. The actors of the HMC and their owners—or what we call "parent organisations"—are presented in the following figure:

In the beginning, the management of the HMC was divided into two entities: the real-estate company and the operating-service company. The operating-service company was a for-profit corporation responsible for the operating services by contracting various companies and people, for

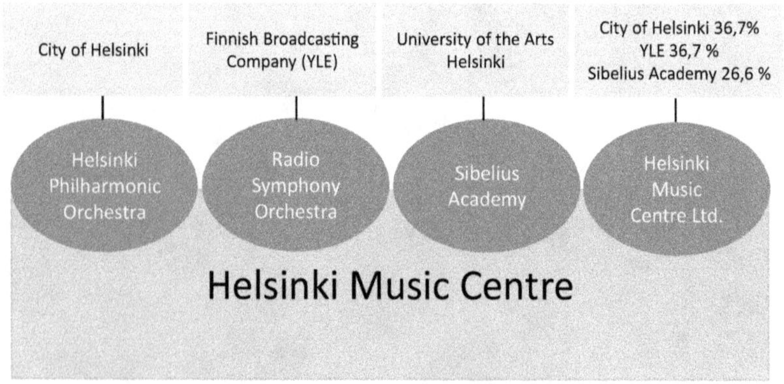

Figure 4.1 The actors and owners of the Helsinki Music Centre

DOI: 10.4324/9780429273919-5

Table 4.1 Overview of the partnering organisations of the Helsinki Music Centre in 2012

	Helsinki Philharmonic Orchestra	*Radio Symphony Orchestra*	*Sibelius Academy*	*Helsinki Music Centre Ltd.*
Established	1883	1927	1882	2010
Size	Musicians: 102 Administration: 11	Musicians: 93 Administration: 9	Students: 1,500 Teaching staff: 180 (full-time), 300 (part-time)	Staff: 11
Activities	80 concerts/year Touring Recording HPO godchildren	70 concerts/year Touring Recording	600 concerts/year University-level music education, research, and artistic activity	Maintenance of the premises Space rental Event production
Type of organisation	Symphony orchestra Part of the Helsinki City organisation	Symphony orchestra Part of the Finnish Broadcasting Company	Music academy Part of the University of the Arts Helsinki	Service organisation Limited Company

example, to run the restaurant, café, and shop, and to provide cleaning, security, technical, and cloakroom services. The table below summarises the activities of the four main actors of the HMC.

Managerial challenge

We were interested in how to manage the organisational identity construction in a newly established cultural joint venture.

Managerial response

In the very beginning of the opening of the cultural joint venture, the four organisations of the HMC—two orchestras, the music university, and the service company—all seemed to share a similar ideal view of the centre. The HMC was envisioned as a place to interact and as a living-room space filled with people and music. They all supported the idea of a swarm of people to fill the centre, not only concertgoers, but also citizens and visitors walking through the centre, having a cup of coffee, enjoying themselves, and, at the same time, being exposed to music. On the other hand, all four organisations seemed to fear that the HMC might turn out to be an empty place, filled with people only at concert events.

Hence, the HMC was seen more as a place to be, interact, and enjoy oneself rather than just another concert hall. In particular, the music university located inside the music centre seemed to face a challenge: the music centre should be more than a concert hall as it also includes a university-level music academy with a range of student activities and genres of music. While classical music remained the main offering of the two symphony orchestras, the university also included concerts in other genres, such as folk, global, and jazz music.

On the other hand, the two orchestras and the university seemed to share a key unifying value: a genuine love for music. The future of the HMC was described in relation to promoting music, creating a place to enhance musical culture, and inviting more people into the world of music. All the partnering organisations emphasised an exceptional concert hall with world-class acoustics, in which classical music would be experienced as never before in Finland.

The unifying value of music also reflected a shared fear that the music centre would lose its identity that was rooted in musical values and become a conference venue. Organisational members of the symphony orchestras felt that music was secondary in their previous locations and that nothing at the HMC should jeopardise the primary focus on music. However, they all welcomed other forms of arts, such as visual-art exhibitions and cross-art events, to engage with the HMC.

Negotiating between local, national, and international identities

The scope of international/national/local identity varied between the main actors of the HMC. One of the symphony orchestras and the university emphasised their national identities and national roles, whereas the other symphony orchestra focused more on its local identity and meaning for the local audiences.

All the organisations involved in the joint venture of HMC had international activities and objectives. For instance, organisational members of the university explained that the music centre was going to be an important "showcase" for a broad range of national and international activities of the university. Along the same line, the members of the service company envisaged an even more international role, with visiting international orchestras and soloists.

Negotiating between artistic content and services

The fourth actor, the for-profit company Helsinki Music Centre Ltd., was responsible for coordinating the outsourced activities, maintaining the building, marketing the centre, providing technical services, and renting out space. However, there seemed to be somewhat conflicting views on the role and tasks of the service organisation. The service organisation was established only a year before the opening of the HMC and was thus a new actor for the partnering organisations. On the one hand, the service organisation was perceived as a key actor aiming to hold power, and on the other, an actor serving the main actors of the HMC.

The service organisation was expected to manage, for example, the cafes and shops, and to provide building maintenance and technical facilities as well as rent out space to various types of clients. Some people expected it to be active in cross-organisational projects (e.g., audience development), while others considered such activities to be the responsibility of the other three main actors of the centre. The organisational members seemed to share the view that the service organisation was different from the others and did not clearly see themselves as sharing an identity with it.

In the beginning, it was natural that it remained rather unclear what kind of identity the service organisation aimed to develop for the HMC. The issue became even more important as the newly appointed CEO of the organisation, who had a background in business, was unfamiliar with music. The other three organisations seemed to be suspicious about any strategic decisions made by the new CEO, who was responsible for the economics and service development of the HMC. The first executive director of the HMC was responsible for some content issues and had a long history in and profound knowledge of music. She had been involved in the music centre project for over 20 years, working closely with the three main actors of the HMC. After the opening of the HMC, a new executive director was selected who had a background in business. Some fears were raised that the new executive director might not share the underlying key value of the "love for music." For instance, the other main actors were worried about the amount of space rented for conference and seminar usage.

This distrust towards the service organisation was reflected in the identity construction. Although the executive director shared the vision of "*a place full of actions and music*," they used a different kind of metaphor for the HMC, referring to it, for instance, as a "*shopping mall.*" This departed somewhat from the metaphor used by the other interviewees as "*a park full of music and people.*" Interestingly, the main actors seemed to share a joint vision of the HMC, but at the same time, they also emphasised their own organisations' established and distinctive identities. This seemed to be a potential source of tension as to whose centre it was and who the main actors were.

There were also differences in the ways organisational members saw the new joint venture as a space or a community based on organisational roles. For example, the marketing and communications personnel seemed to refer to the new music centre as a community even before the actual opening, whereas the management of the partnering organisations emphasised the existing organisational identities and perceived the HMC mainly as a space. For the two symphony orchestras, maintaining their distinct identities was perceived even as a survival issue: if they were not different, why have two orchestras? On the other hand, symphony orchestras in the same city had to coordinate their concert schedules and contents regardless of the shared or not shared facilities. From the university point of view, the emphasis on the HMC as a concert hall seemed to build tension between the tasks as a concert provider and as a music university.

4.2. Case 2: The Grand National Theater of Peru, Lima, Peru

The Grand National Theater of Peru is a multipurpose theatre and concert hall in Lima, Peru, designed by the architects Alfonso de la Piedra and José Nepomuceno. The theatre is part of the *Cultural Tridium*, Peru's biggest performing arts centre, and is equipped with a main hall with 1,500 seats. The theatre opened in 2012 and was the much awaited home of Peru's Symphony Orchestra, National Ballet, and National Chorus. In addition, the Grand National Theater of Peru houses the National Children's Chorus and the National Folkloric Ensemble and is located next to the National Library of Peru and the Museo de la Nación.

Managerial challenge

We were interested in how to manage the contested national identities of a cultural joint venture with a national mission.

Managerial response

The Grand National Theater of Peru has a dual leadership model of programming and managerial leaders and is closely supervised by the Ministry of Culture. The head of programming is responsible for the marketing and audience development as well. The managerial leader is mainly responsible for administration and technical and facility management. Each of the music ensembles manages its own marketing, and, for example, social media sites.

Thus, it seems that the organisation is closer to a siloed than a networked one. Moreover, the ensembles do not share practice facilities, which makes informally sharing knowledge difficult and impedes building a joint identity.

The Grand National Theater of Peru seemed to face a challenge around multiple interests and expectations. Its identity construction has been torn between its national identity connected to the request to perform Peru's folk music and the request to perform Western classical music. The managerial implications of a case represent how organisations graft institutional elements onto their identity to garner legitimacy (e.g., Glynn, 2008), while identity filters institutional demands and affects the way expectations are infused into organisations (Kraatz & Block, 2008).

Organisational structure and culture—identifying organisational identities

The Grand National Theater of Peru had a dual leadership model of programming and managerial leaders. In addition, the Ministry of Culture closely supervised its operations. The head of programming was responsible also for the marketing and audience development. The managerial leader was mainly responsible for the administration and the technical and facility management. Each of the music ensembles also had its own marketing, and, for example, social media sites. Thus, it seemed that the organisation was closer to a siloed than a networked structure of cooperation. Moreover, the ensembles did not seem to share the theatre's rehearsal facilities, which made the sharing of information and knowledge difficult and also impeded the joint identity construction.

Perceived brand identity and co-branding strategy

In the Grand National Theater of Peru, the brand identity was mainly connected to the nation, with close connection to the Ministry of Culture. The joint venture also had a strong profile in classical performances, but not in folklore. The internal identity was built on the space, as it was pointed out that it did not seem to create a sense of community. Thus, we propose to categorise the joint venture's brand identity under the house of brands. Yet, the strong role of the nation in branding still needs to be emphasised.

4.3 Case 3: Seattle Opera and Seattle Symphony, Seattle, USA

Founded in 1963, Seattle Opera is one of the leading opera companies in the United States. In August of 2003, the company inaugurated its new state-of-the-art home, Marion Oliver McCaw Hall, located on the Seattle Center campus, in the heart of the arts and cultural district of the city. At the end of 2018, the company planned to move its education, artistic, and administrative programs to a new civic home next to McCaw Hall. The new building will be an accessible community resource and will allow the company to expand its education programmes.

Seattle Symphony was established in 1903 and is a vital part of the Pacific Northwest cultural scene, recognised for its extraordinary performances, programming, recordings, and community engagement. In 1998, the Seattle Symphony inaugurated its new home, Benaroya Hall, noted for its architectural and acoustical splendour. Three years later, the orchestra opened *Soundbridge* Seattle Symphony Music Discovery Center, where people of all ages explore the world of symphonic music through exhibits, classes, and live music presentations. In 2019, the orchestra renovated and reopened the space as the Octave 9: Raisbeck Music Center, an immersive environment for inventive performances, education opportunities, and community engagement.

Managerial challenge

We were interested in how to manage the practical conflicts at the beginning of a new cultural joint venture.

Managerial response

At the beginning of the joint venture, the two organisations were located in the same building, causing many practical issues in their everyday lives. For example, the rehearsal times of the halls were considered challenging to share between the different organisations, which greatly affected their work.

The managerial implications of the case include a recommendation to identify the tensions and sometimes even conflicting values that people may hold simultaneously. Acknowledging this contradiction helps managers to tackle the issue in practice. The individuals' capacity to hold a set of identities as well as the organisations' ability to build on these multilayered identities are important managerial implications, particularly with regards to creating a joint community with shared values (such as the love for music), norms, and practices. If arts managers can specify the various identities and their meeting points, it can help cultural organisations avoid conflicts. Also, an understanding of the various levels of identities and values underneath the different practices enables managers to attend to the values that facilitate organisational change more efficiently.

Moreover, the managers should note that shared practices enable the building of shared identities, engagement, and commitment in cultural joint ventures. Especially at the beginning of a joint effort, several shared practices should be created in order to provide a place for the different actors to meet and get to know each other. For example, jointly produced events on a topic that interests all the participants (e.g., family engagement and fundraising) might work well as a first initiative towards a community with shared organisational identities.

References

Albert, S., & Whetten, D. A. (1985). Organizational identity. In B. M. Staw & L. L. Cummings (Eds.), *Research in organizational behavior* (pp. 263–295, Volume 7). Greenwich: JAI Press.

Alvesson, M. (2003). Interpretive unpacking: Moderately destabilizing identities and images in organisation studies. In E. A. Locke (Ed.), *Postmodernism and management: Pros, cons and the alternative* (pp. 3–27). Oxford: Elsevier Ltd.

Alvesson, M., Ashcraft, K. L., & Thomas, R. (2008). Identity matters: Reflections on the construction of identity scholarship in organisation studies. *Organisation, 15*(1), 5–28.

Anttonen, R., Ateca-Amestoy, V., Holopainen, K., Johansson, T., Jyrämä, A., Karkkunen, A., Kiitsak-Prikk, K., Kuznetsova-Bodanovitš, K., Luonila, M., Kõlar, J-M., Plaza, B., Pulk, K., Pusa, T., Ranczakowska-Ljutjuk, A., Sassi, M., Stiller, I., & Äyväri, A. (2016). *Managing art projects with societal impact: Study book for students, stakeholders and researchers*. Helsinki: Unigrafia.

Ashforth, B. E., & Mael, F. (1989). Social identity theory and the organization. *Academy of Management Review, 14*(1), 20–39.

Ashforth, B. E., Harrison, S. H., & Corley, K. G. (2008). Identification in organizations: An examination of four fundamental questions. *Journal of management, 34*(3), 325–374.

Atewologun, D., Kutzer, R., Doldor, E., Anderson, D., & Sealy, R. (2017). Individual-level foci of identification at work: A systematic review of the literature. *International Journal of Management Reviews, 19*(3), 273–295.

Beech, N., Gilmore, C., Cochrane, E., & Greig, G. (2012). Identity work as a response to tensions: A re-narration in opera rehearsals. *Scandinavian Journal of Management, 28*(1), 39–47.

Beech, N., & Huxham, C. (2003). Cycles of identity formation in interorganisational collaboration. *International Studies of Management, 33*(3), 28–52.

Brewer, M. B., & Gardner, W. (1996). Who is this "We"? Levels of collective identity and self representations. *Journal of Personality and Social Psychology, 71*(1), 83.

Brown, A. D. (2017). Identity work and organizational identification. *International Journal of Management Reviews, 19*(3), 296–317.

Clark, S. M., Gioia, D. A., Ketchen, D. J., & Thomas, J. B. (2010). Transitional identity as a facilitator of organisational identity change during a merger. *Administrative Science Quarterly, 55*(2), 397–438.

Clegg, S. R., Rhodes, C., & Kornberger, M. (2007). Desperately seeking legitimacy: Organisational identity and emerging industries. *Organisation Studies*, *28*(4), 495–513.

Cloutier, C., & Ravasi, D. (2020). Identity trajectories: Explaining long-term patterns of continuity and change in organisational identities. *Academy of Management Journal*, *63*(4), 1196–1235.

Collinson, J. A. (2006). Just 'non-academics'? Research administrators and contested occupational identity. *Work, Employment and Society*, *20*(2), 267–288.

Corley, K. G., & Gioia, D. A. (2004). Identity ambiguity and change in the wake of a corporate spin-off. *Administrative Science Quarterly*, *49*(1), 173–208.

Corley, K. G., Harquail, C. V., Pratt, M. G., Glynn, M. A., Fiol, C. M., & Hatch, M. J. (2006). Guiding organizational identity through aged adolescence. *Journal of Management Inquiry*, *15*(2), 85–99.

Cornelissen, J. P. (2002). On the 'organizational identity' metaphor. *British Journal of Management*, *13*(3), 259–268.

Cornelissen, J. P., Haslam, S. A., & Balmer, J. M. (2007). Social identity, organizational identity and corporate identity: Towards an integrated understanding of processes, patternings and products. *British Journal of Management*, *18*, S1–S16.

Dutton, J. E., & Dukerich, J. M. (1991). Keeping an eye on the mirror: Image and identity in organizational adaptation. *Academy of Management Journal, 34*(3), 517–554.

Dutton, J. E., Dukerich, J. M., & Harquail, C. V. (1994). Organizational images and member identification. *Administrative science quarterly*, 239–263.

Fiol, C. M., Hatch, M. J., & Golden-Biddle, K. (1998). Organizational culture and identity: What's the difference anyway?" In D. Whetten & P. Godfrey (Eds.), *Identity in organizations. Building theory through conversation* (pp. 56–59). Thousand Oaks, CA: SAGE.

Gioia, D. A., & Chittipeddi, K. (1991). Sensemaking and sensegiving in strategic change initiation. *Strategic Management Journal*, *12*(6), 433–448.

Gioia, D. A., Price, K. N., Hamilton, A. L., & Thomas, J. B. (2010). Forging an identity: An insider-outsider study of processes involved in the formation of organisational identity. *Administrative Science Quarterly*, *55*(1), 1–46.

Gioia, D. A., Schultz, M., & Corley, K. G. (2000). Organizational identity, image, and adaptive instability. *Academy of Management Review*, *25*(1), 63–81.

Gioia, D. A., Schultz, M., & Corley, K. G. (2002). On celebrating the organizational identity metaphor: A rejoinder to Cornelissen. *British Journal of Management*, *13*(3), 269–275.

Gioia, D. A., & Thomas, J. B. (1996). Identity, image, and issue interpretation: Sensemaking during strategic change in academia. *Administrative Science Quarterly*, *41*, 370–403.

Glynn, M. A. (2008). Beyond constraint: How institutions enable identities. *The Sage Handbook of Organizational Institutionalism*, *41*, 3–430.

Glynn, M. A., & Abzug, R. (2002). Institutionalizing identity: Symbolic isomorphism and organizational names. *Academy of Management Journal, 45*(1), 267–280.

Golden-Biddle, K., & Rao, H. (1997). Breaches in the boardroom: Organisational identity and conflicts of commitment in a nonprofit organisation. *Organisation Science*, *8*, 593–611.

Haslam, S. A. (2004). *Psychology in organizations*. London: SAGE.

Haslam, S. A., & Ellemers, N. (2005). Social identity in industrial and organizational psychology: Concepts, controversies and contributions. *International Review of Industrial and Organizational Psychology*, *20*(1), 39–118.

Hatch, M. J., & Schultz, M. (1997). Relations between organizational culture, identity and image. *European Journal of Marketing, 31*(5–6), 356–365.

Hatch, M. J., & Schultz, M. (2002). The dynamics of organisational identity. *Human Relations*, *55*(8), 989–1018.

Hatch, M. J., & Schultz, M. (2008). *Taking brand initiative: How to align vision, culture and identity through corporate branding.* San Francisco, CA: Jossey-Bass/Wiley.

Hogg, M. A., & Terry, D. J. (2000). The dynamic, diverse, and variable faces of organizational identity. *Academy of Management Review*, *25*(1), 150–152.

Johansson, T., & Jyrämä, A. (2016). Network of organizational identities in the formation of a cultural joint venture: A case study of the Helsinki Music Centre. *International Journal of Arts Management*, 67–78.

Klein, J., & Amis, H. M. (2018). Design change and the emergence of pluralistic identities. *Academy of Management Proceedings, 1.*

Kraatz, M. S., & Block, E. S. (2008). Organizational implications of institutional pluralism. *The Sage Handbook of Organizational Institutionalism*, *840*, 243–275.

Noh, S., & Tolbert, P. S. (2019). Organisational identities of U.S. art museums and audience reactions. *Poetics*, *72*, 94–107.

Onishi, T. (2019). Venture philanthropy and practice variations: The interplay of institutional logics and organisational identities. *Nonprofit and Voluntary Sector Quarterly*, 1–25.

Parker, M. (2007). Identification: Organisations and structuralism. In A. Pullen, N. Beech, & D. Sims (Eds.), *In exploring identity: Concepts and methods* (pp. 61–68). New York: Palgrave Macmillan.

Pratt, M. G. (2018). Hybrid and multiple organisational identities. In M. G. Pratt, M. Schultz, B. E. Ashforth, & D. Ravasi (Eds.), *The Oxford handbook of organisational identity* (pp. 106–120). New York: Oxford University Press.

Ravasi, D., & Schultz, M. (2006). Responding to organisational identity threats: Exploring the role of organisational culture. *Academy of Management Journal*, *49*(3), 433–458.

Ravasi, D., & Van Rekom, J. (2003). Key issues in organizational identity and identification theory. *Corporate Reputation Review*, *6*(2), 118–132.

Sluss, D. M., & Ashforth, B. E. (2007). Relational identity and identification: Defining ourselves through work relationships. *Academy of management review, 32*(1), 9–32.

Tienari, J., & Vaara, E. (2016). Identity construction in mergers and acquisitions: A discursive sensemaking perspective. In M. G. Pratt, M. Schultz, B. E. Ashforth, & D. Ravasi (Eds.), *The Oxford handbook of organizational identity* (pp. 455–473). Oxford: Oxford University Press.

Tuori, A., & Vilén, T. (2011). Subject positions and power relations in creative organizations: Taking a discursive view on organizational creativity. *Creativity and Innovation Management*, *20*(2), 90–99.

Van Knippenberg, D. (2016). Making sense of who we are: Leadership and organizational identity. In M. G. Pratt, M. Schultz, B. E. Ashforth, & D. Ravasi (Eds.), *The Oxford handbook of organizational identity* (pp. 335–349). Oxford: Oxford University Press.

Vilén, T. (2010). *Being in between: An ethnographic study of opera and dialogical identity construction*. Helsinki: Edita.

Weick, K. E. (1995). *Sensemaking in organizations*. Thousand Oaks, CA: SAGE.

Wohlstetter, P., Smith, J., & Malloy, C. L. (2005). Strategic alliances in action: Toward a theory of evolution. *The Policy Studies Journal*, *33*(3), 419–442.

Yanow, D. (2003). Seeing organisational learning: A cultural view. In D. Nicolini, S. Gherardi, & D. Yanow (Eds.), *In knowing in organisations. A practice-based approach*. New York: ME Sharpy.

Ybema, S., Keenoy, T., Oswick, C., Beverungen, A., Ellis, N., & Sabelis, I. (2009). Articulating identities. *Human Relations*, *62*(3), 299–322.

Part II

Managing the multiple images and brand relationships of cultural joint ventures

Part II adopts a new perspective and looks at the phenomenon of cultural joint ventures from the perspective of image and branding. First, we provide an overview of the current discussions about branding, namely brand identity and image in the context of joint ventures. In the subchapters, we provide insights into what tools are currently used to develop multiple brands and how these tools can be adapted for use in cultural joint ventures. Second, we discuss novel approaches and tools for managing multiple brands. We build on the tools previously identified, provide new insights for their use in the context of cultural joint ventures, and present new ways to evaluate and manage brands. Finally, Part II focuses on cases that highlight and exemplify the findings, tools, and insights presented in the earlier chapters.

DOI: 10.4324/9780429273919-6

5 Multiple brand identities and images in cultural joint ventures

5.1. Current understandings of brand images

The aim of a brand identity is to enable the identification of, for example, a product, company, city, or person from other similar ones. It aims to create a profile, a distinct identity for the products of a company or the company itself. In today's world, it is hard to find any product or company without a brand; even such everyday products as carrots or potatoes have different profiles, creating an image for that particular type of vegetable. If everyday products have distinct brand identities, this is even more the case with cultural products. In fact, branding is a vital element for arts and cultural organisations (Colbert, 2009; Kotler & Scheff, 1997). There is an ongoing debate around the use of marketing/business instruments in the context of art; however, we argue that even if the notion of a brand might be rejected, the actual process of branding, that of building a distinct brand identity, is inherent in all artistic activities (see Colbert, 2009; Scheff & Kotler, 1996). Indeed, one could argue that in the arts, creating a distinct profile or image has always been present. This image is created, for example, through a particular type of expression, identified by an artist's name and style.

Brand is often defined as a name, signal, term, symbol design, or combinations of these, by which a product, service, or organisation can be identified (Anholt, 2009; Jyrämä et al., 2015; Keller & Lehmann, 2006). Creating a brand identity enables customers, audiences, and other stakeholders to recognise and remember the product or company in relation to its competitors. Its aim is to encourage consumers and other stakeholders to create a bond, a relationship with the product or company, and thus motivate the desired behaviour, for example, purchasing art works or sponsoring the organisation (see Balmer, 1995). Hence, a brand identity is more than just the features of a product or service, but a deeper way to portray its special character or identity and build a relationship between this identity and the consumer, through both functional and emotional elements (see Kapferer, 2004).

DOI: 10.4324/9780429273919-7

Brand identity is the way an organisation aims to be profiled. It is the internal perspective of what organisations wish to be, how they desire to be unique and recognised by their customers and other stakeholders (e.g., Balmer, 2001; Janonis et al., 2007). Brand management can be seen as the activity seeking to build the organisation's desire for identity. Brand image, on the other hand, refers to the customers' perceptions and interpretations of this identity (e.g., Aaker & Joachimsthaler, 2000a; Keller, 1993, 2012; Park et al., 1986).

Brand image has been defined through various elements, such as brand loyalty, brand love, brand attitude, brand associations, attractiveness, brand identification, behavioural expectations, brand personality, brand person, and brand equity. These dimensions represent different ways to understand how customers relate to the brand. Each dimension captures different aspects yet coalesces into a holistic view of brand image (see Hsieh et al., 2004; see also Aaker, 1991, 1996; Hieke, 2010; Jyrämä et al., 2015). Next, we provide a short overview of some key dimensions and their interconnections.

Brand personality (associations) is a way to analyse a brand and its image through similar characteristics one could use to analyse a person's personality. The brand personality is described by sets of adjectives that portray its image and distinctiveness (Aaker, 1997). **Brand attitude** refers to the consumer's evaluation and judgment of the brand. Usually, the brand attitude is either positive or negative, affecting, for example, the choice of brand (see Janonis et al., 2007; Jyrämä et al., 2015; Peter & Olson, 2005). The conceptualisation of **brand loyalty** is a mixture of attitudinal and behavioural elements combining both functional and emotional elements (for more discussion, see Punniyamoorthy & Prasanna Mohan Raj, 2007). For example, brand loyalty can relate to a sense of ease, in that our repeated selection of certain products makes our everyday life easier. Originally, brand loyalty was defined as repeated purchases by customers, for example always selecting the same brands of bread. Later, an attitudinal aspect was added (Oliver, 1999, p. 34), after which brand loyalty was seen to build via relationships in the sense of how the brand image reflects one's own identity in terms of lifestyle choices, for example attending the same summer festivals year after year.

Brand love emphasises the relationship between consumer and brand, as it assesses satisfied consumers' passionate emotional attachment to particular brands (Batra et al., 2012; Carroll & Ahuvia, 2006; Chaudhuri & Holbrook, 2001). **Brand identification** captures the consumer's own identity vis-à-vis the brand. It aims to understand how a brand can become part of a person's own identity. For example, a consumer may feel that criticism or praise towards a brand feels like criticism towards oneself (He & Li, 2010; Marin et al., 2008). **Identity attractiveness** looks at the brand relationship through comparisons with other brands (Marin & Ruiz, 2006; Marin et al., 2008). **Brand equity** adopts a different perspective in looking at a brand, focusing on the financial perspective and evaluating the value of a brand in monetary ways, rather than focusing on the relationship between brand and consumer. Brand equity analysis looks at the various brands and their value vis-à-vis the value of the company's other assets, such as equipment or buildings. (see Aaker, 1991).

It is noteworthy to point out that these dimensions of brand image are only a selection. The literature presents even more ways to determine what constitutes a brand image such as presented in the following figure.

The selected elements relating to brand image described above and shown in Figure 5.1 are important topics for managers to reflect on when

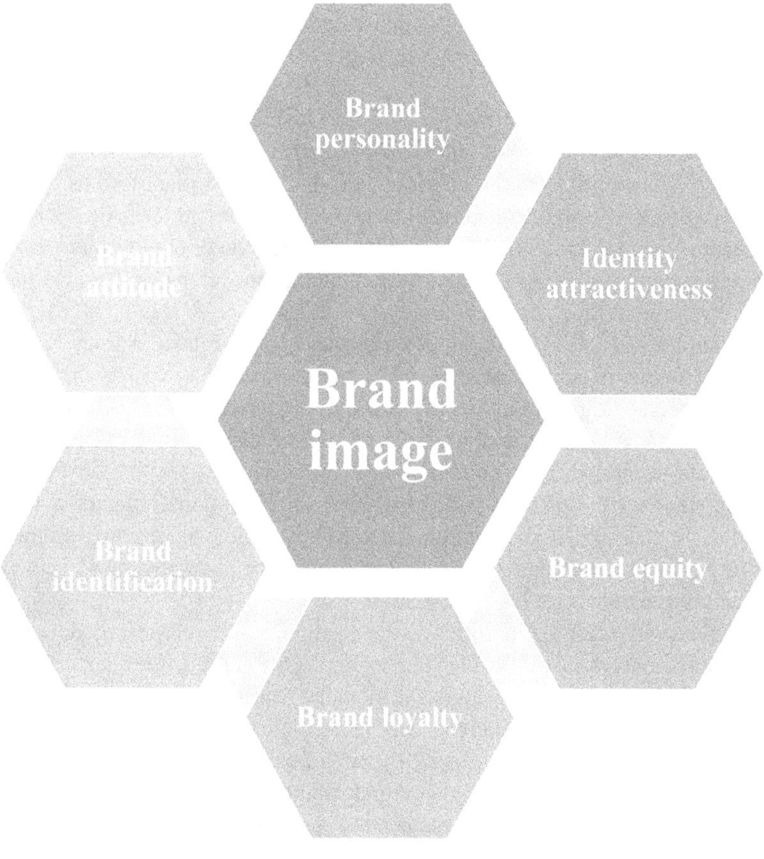

Figure 5.1 A selection of brand image dimensions

building brand identity internally. They represent several perspectives to adopt at the brand management level when building a brand identity and image. These brand dimensions have been explored in the context of art in several studies. Next, we present some selected examples of these studies followed by a case example on managerial implications.

Brand personality has been studied, for example, in the context of a customer's ability to differentiate between theatre and other cultural venues (Colbert & St-James, 2014). Brand personality has been combined with use image, how product service is used and focuses on its functionality, arts image, focus on artistic quality, and curator/manager image with professionals to look at the brand as a person in a museum context (Pusa & Uusitalo, 2014). Brand personality has also been connected to the values of, for example, a cultural organisation or a tourist destination (Camarero et al., 2010), for example honesty and nurturance in a nonprofit context (Venable et al., 2005). Understanding customer perceptions of brand personality provides the means for a manager to build customer relationships further with the brand.

Brand attitude, brand loyalty, and brand love all look at the customers' relationships with a brand. Brand loyalty is also one of the most studied concepts of branding in the cultural field. It has been identified as a way for a manager to understand and create customer retention, as a tool for customer segmentation and the building of patronage or commitment to art organisations, and as an element for managing sponsorship in the arts, just to name a few (Mazodier & Merunka, 2012; Swanson & Davis, 2006).

Brand identification in cultural fields can manifest itself in many ways, for example a person being a fan of a band or a patron of an arts organisation. Understanding brand identification, or organisational identification, is one of the key managerial tools for maintaining and building art patronage programmes. Brand identification relates to the commitment of patrons and understanding the patrons and their brand identification elements to help build, for example, brand communities and sustainable patron programmes. The patronage may manifest itself also through the phenomenon of being a "fan" (see Swanson & Davis, 2006).

The brand equity of a cultural organisation builds on various determinants (Camarero et al., 2011). For example, in cultural tourism, namely in the context of art exhibitions, it includes four dimensions: past visitor loyalty, brand image, perceived quality of the exhibition, and the event's brand values (Camarero et al., 2010). Brand equity analysis allows for the discovery of, for example, a greater understanding of what drives customer satisfaction and the basis for organisation revenues.

We have discussed branding irrespective of the various layers, for example product and company, but there are clear differences when building a brand for different levels. Creating a corporate, organisational brand is more complex than product branding, since the organisation or corporation might encompass several products (Baker & Balmer, 1997). For example, the company employees and leadership build the brand identity through their values and practices (Balmer, 1995; King, 1991). The challenges of branding become even more multiple when cultural joint ventures are considered.

Thus, we now move from discussing the elements of brand image to the focus of the book, which is building brand portfolios and co-branding, and look at the interrelationships of various brands at the organisational level. At the same time, we will connect these to the previously discussed individual brand elements by elaborating on the brand image dimensions. Next, we focus on co-branding and, in particular, on brand architecture.

6 How to manage and join multiple brands

Branding refers not only to building one's identity or image but also to extending brands, connecting existing brands, and co-branding, which means joining two or more brand images together. Especially in the context of joint ventures, decisions about the interrelationships between different brands and their identities are important. Next, we introduce some tools and models that can help to position the brand within the organisation and with the (new) joint venture.

6.1 Brand extension

Brand extension means the transfer of the brand, name, or image to another product or service in order to facilitate faster adoption of the new product or service. The familiar brand name or image created recognition, thus facilitating the transfer of its assumed qualities to the new product. Del Barrio-García and Prados-Peña (2019) discuss the need for authenticity in the brand extension. In order for the successful transfer of the quality to occur, the new product/service needs to be authentic in order to create a perception or experience in the minds of the consumers that is similar to the original brand. Gombault and Selles (2018) point out the need for the brand owner to ensure the legitimacy and quality of the extension. They show the different dimensions in relation to how the Louvre aimed to maintain the authenticity of the Louvre Abu Dhabi brand extension. Among other factors, they mention the architecture, scientific quality, and support for the museum management as the means to ensure the future quality and authenticity of the Louvre brand extension.

One cultural brand that is well known and widely extended is the UNESCO World Heritage List, which provides legitimacy and authenticity for various types of heritage sites throughout the world. Del Barrio-García and Prados-Peña (2019, p. 19) propose that in such a context, the brand extension's "influence of the authenticity variable on the formation of brand

DOI: 10.4324/9780429273919-8

equity for the extension is not *always* significant, but rather depends on the extent of the tourist's previous experience of the heritage site and the degree of knowledge they possess regarding the product category to which the heritage brand extension belongs."

One of the most famous brand extensions in the museum sector, and in the context of culture at large, is the case of Guggenheim. Gombault and Sellers (2018) suggest that the strategic goal of Guggenheim as a private foundation is to build economic growth through brand extensions. Guggenheim has several success stories in their brand extensions, such as Guggenheim Venice, and the famed Guggenheim Bilbao (see Plaza, 2008). On the other hand, they have also encountered failure in creating a brand extension, sometimes having to close down their museums in different locations (see Gombault & Selles, 2018; Ritvala et al., 2021).

One of the main criticisms of these cultural brand extensions on the global level has been the neglect of local actors. It is feared that the global brand will take away customers and content from the local milieu, for example museums. It is hence noteworthy to reflect on why an organisation uses the brand extension strategy to establish itself as a new competitor in local markets rather than create joint ventures with local actors. The key differences between the brand extension strategy and the brand alliance strategy are discussed further on.

6.2 Co-branding

Co-branding means joining brand images together. It often aims to combine two qualities that customers appreciate in the different brands. In everyday life, we can witness these combinations of different brands, such as ice cream and candy, or the addition of a feature, such as Gore-Tex to clothing or shoe brands. Similarly, some brands are joined in the product brand using a particular component, such as Intel with the HP computer brand. The literature on branding has elaborated on the brand identities and images of co-branded products and organisations extensively (Aaker & Joachimsthaler, 2000b; Harish, 2008; Johansson & Jyrämä, 2016). However, it is noteworthy that co-branding focuses especially on the brand level, through a joining of the brand images, and is rarely related to products or organisations joining in other ways, i.e., co-branding may happen in the context of joint ventures, but it occurs often at the brand level, without formal organisational integration, as a collaborative activity.

In the cultural sector, we see co-branding at the product level, for example in the joining of museum brands with designer brands, such as in museum store products. The keys for successful brand extension are the connection between the product and brand image, the expectations of consumers in terms of the fit between the product extension and the brand, and the simplicity of the extended product (see d'Astous et al., 2007).

In addition, co-branding takes place at the organisational level, which is the joining of two cultural organisation brands into one, for example when organising concerts at museum premises, combining the orchestra brand with the museum brand (see d'Astous et al., 2007), with the aim of reaching new target groups from both the music and heritage fields.

When a new joint venture begins, the new entity most likely has several brands or at least a few company brands. Several questions then need to be asked: What brand do we have? How are these brands similar or different? Do they serve the same cultural segments or not? What brands do we wish to keep? Do we wish to have one or several new brands?

The branding in joint ventures tackles the management of a multitude of brands simultaneously by one organisation or company, thus creating a brand portfolio that fits well, complements, and supports the different brands rather than a mix of brands that potentially disturbs the brand relationship consumers have with the individual brands. The same tools, brand portfolio or brand architecture for example, can be used when managing the brand portfolio of a new joint venture. The two main ways to view brand mix are from the brand portfolio and brand architecture perspectives.

6.3 Brand portfolio

The brand portfolio includes all the brands and sub-brands attached to product-market offerings, and the brand architecture provides a tool to analyse and manage the brand portfolio by specifying the roles of brands and the nature of the relationships between brands and various product-market contexts (Aaker & Joachimsthaler, 2000b; Harish, 2008; see also Jyrämä et al., 2015). Brand portfolios consist of specific dimensions, namely how many brands, how many customer segments, and how to position the brands. The literature provides arguments for selecting a concentration of a few brands as well as for a multitude of brands in a portfolio. The views on brand complementary versus competitiveness are various and include the following: creating a strong market presence and building barriers to entry by competing brands in one's own brand portfolio, and not cannibalising one's own brand but creating a brand that can devour your market share or creating complementary brand portfolios (Morgan & Rego, 2009). Complementary and competing dichotomies are related to the target segments, which raises the question: do we aim for the same customers or different ones with the other respective brands?

Similarly, there are several views on the decision-making with regard to target segments. On the one hand, selecting different target segments for different brands avoids internal brand competition, while on the other hand, it might create uncertainty in the minds of the consumers around the overall brand image(s) and their fit, as well as the company brand (Morgan & Rego, 2009; see also Kim et al., 2018), and even more so in joint ventures with two or more organisational brand images. The third dimension to reflect on after deciding on the scope of the brand and the target segments is brand portfolio positioning, that is, evaluating the price-quality perceptions of a brand by the consumers. Achieving a broad brand portfolio at different price-quality levels allows for a larger market share but can be costly. In addition, as with the target segments, the overall organisational brand might get blurred due to several perceptions of the quality the organisation is offering. Moreover, the costs and needed resources for a broad brand portfolio might outweigh its benefits (Morgan & Rego, 2009; Brunner & Baum, 2020).

In addition, brand loyalty plays an important role in the ways we relate to brands. We might have a strong commitment to a brand, whereby it becomes part of our identity and our lifestyle, or it might be only a way to make everyday decisions easier, and thus constitutes a functional relationship (see Aaker, 1991, 1996; Jyrämä, 2017; Lindroos et al., 2005). The brand loyalty also may build on emotional ties, referred to as brand love (Batra et al., 2012), or it may be a mundane one that is not even consciously realised. In the joint-venture context, the brand loyalty comes under scrutiny: how do customers relate to the new (joint) identity of the brand?

We suggest that in managing a brand portfolio, each brand's target group brand image, in terms of quality and price, should be categorised with an evaluation of the consumers' brand commitment and brand loyalty. The following figure illustrates the different levels, with examples from the cultural sector.

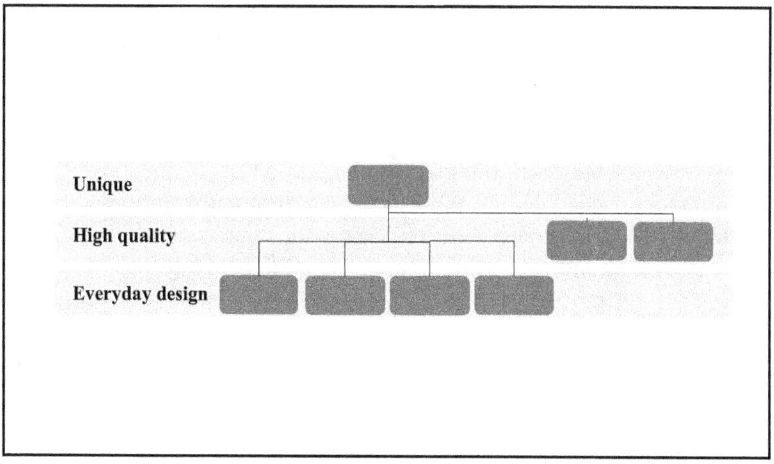

Figure 6.1 Brand portfolio levels

Brand portfolio analysis looks at the portfolio to detect differences, for example, in terms of the homogeneity vs. heterogeneity of the brands within the portfolio. Usually, the brand portfolio is viewed at the product brand level, focusing mainly on the number of brands in a portfolio without looking at their relationships with the corporate brand (Gabrielli & Baghi, 2020). Next, we introduce the concept of brand architecture, a managerial tool for brand portfolio management, especially focusing on the product-corporate level of brand relationships.

6.4 Brand architecture

Brand architecture looks at the brand portfolio from the perspective of the brands' relative power positions. It is especially useful in a joint-venture context in which existing brands are forced to relate to each other, in comparison to brand portfolios developed in one organisation, where each existing brand is considered while new ones are created.

The Brand Relations Spectrum (BRS), introduced by Aaker and Joachimsthaler (2000a, 2000b; see also Jyrämä et al., 2015), offers four branding strategies to establish the brand power relationships. The BRS focuses on the relationship of the product brands to the organisation's overall brand. Brand architecture identifies the relevant power positions and relationships between the brands. The brand with a stronger position is considered to be the endorser brand and the sub-brand the endorsed one (Aaker & Joachimsthaler, 2000; see discussion also Jyrämä et al., 2015).

The branding strategies are referred to as brand architecture strategies. The main ones are 1) house of brands, 2) endorsed brands, 3) sub-brands, and 4) branded house (Aaker & Joachimsthaler, 2000b; see discussion also Jyrämä et al., 2015). Next, we elaborate on each strategy and give examples from the arts field.

1) House of brands means that the individual brands are managed separately, in which the organisational/company brand has a weak position and is not emphasised. The aim is to create strong brand positions for individual brands. This strategy is often used with companies who have large brand portfolios and whose brands are competing rather than complementing ones.

An example in the arts field is the choice of some major record companies not to emphasise the company brand, or record label, but instead to mainly focus on the individual product brands, i.e., branding the music groups or musicians in their marketing communications. However, smaller record companies, i.e., independent record labels, usually do not follow the house of brands brand-architecture strategy, but quite the opposite, which is the branded house strategy emphasising the company's brand or record label (see the discussion on independent labels, e.g., Lee, 1995). In addition, the main brands often acquire these independent labels and continue to benefit from their brand image instead of merging them with their own brand, in order to ensure that the brand community remains loyal.

2) Endorsed brands describe a brand architecture strategy in which the organisational brand is connected to the individual brands, but not emphasised. The endorsed brand architecture strategy allows for building some confidence in the brand in consumers' minds, yet at the same time, having brands with independent brand images and even maintaining competing brands in the brand portfolio.

As discussed above, some record companies and, for example, publishing houses maintain an endorsed brand architecture strategy, emphasising authors or artists as the main brand names and keeping the company brand secondary. The endorsed brand architecture strategy may include several "endorsement levels." A good example is the publishing house at the company-level Gummerus, the book series for quality books called the Yellow Library, and then the author's and book's name at the final product level, distinguishing the actual item in question. Hence, they adopt the endorsed brand strategy.

3) Sub-brand is a brand architecture strategy whereby each individual brand is connected to the organisational brand, but with a co-brand image. The sub-brand architecture strategy enables new brands to enter the market faster as the brand already has familiarity and brand relationship with the consumers.

The design industry provides several examples of sub-brands as a brand architecture strategy. Strong design brands in fabrics or ceramics use the company brand when introducing new series or models to the market but give each new design its own brand as well. This enables the passing of the existing brand image on to the new brand extensions as seen, for example, in the connection between the brands of Marimekko and Arabia.

4) Branded house means that the brand architecture strategy positions the company's product brand(s) as unified under the main company/organisational brand. In this architecture strategy, the communication and brand image build mainly on the organisational level, where the individual product brands function as tools for the organisational brands.

A good example is a theatre with a strong identity, where the various theatre productions fall under the theatre's organisational brand. Similarly, many performing-arts organisations, such as opera houses, festivals, and dance companies, position their individual "products" as performances under the strong organisational brand, thus contributing to the productions their unique individual brand images as part of this larger brand. Often, museums with changing exhibitions follow the branded house brand architecture strategy. In opera houses, for example, the opera and ballet sides often have their own organisations and brands, yet the productions are marketed through the main brand. In contrast, in many museums, the sub-brands are put forward as the main brands rather than the national gallery or exhibitions as such.

Jyrämä et al. (2015) included a fifth strategy, whereby the sub-brands in the portfolio endorse the organisational/company-level brands, called the endorsed house strategy.

5) Endorsed house brand architecture strategy was identified when analysing the Helsinki Music Centre as a cultural joint venture at its early stage. The endorsed house brand architecture strategy builds the joint-brand image by emphasising the brand images entering the joint venture. In this strategy, the endorsing brands are at a lower level, while the brand image is created at a higher level.

At its early stage of the Helsinki Music Centre, its existing strong organisational brand images, namely the Helsinki City Philharmonic, Radio Symphony Orchestra, and Sibelius Academy, jointly created the content and image for the Centre, thus endorsing the house brand. This brand architecture strategy can be used in other joint ventures as well in order to keep the brand commitments for the existing brands. However, the brand architecture strategies may change as the company strategy or consumer attitudes towards the brands change. For example, a shift from the house of brands strategy towards the brand architecture strategies connecting to the corporate level has been noted (Gabrielli & Baghi, 2020) as a means to build stronger brand equity and an efficient brand management system. Brand architecture strategies can also be used when reflecting on the relationships between brands with separate services at the "umbrella level"; examples of this include a city's various services, such as libraries, schools, etc., which have relationships with the city brand, or the relationship between an organisation and its departments, or among various stakeholder groups, for example in the university context (e.g., Leijerholt et al., 2019; Spry et al., 2020).

We will return to the brand architecture strategies in the next chapter to elaborate on them specifically in the cultural-joint-venture context. For a summary of the brand architecture strategies within the relevant cultural sectors, please see the following figure:

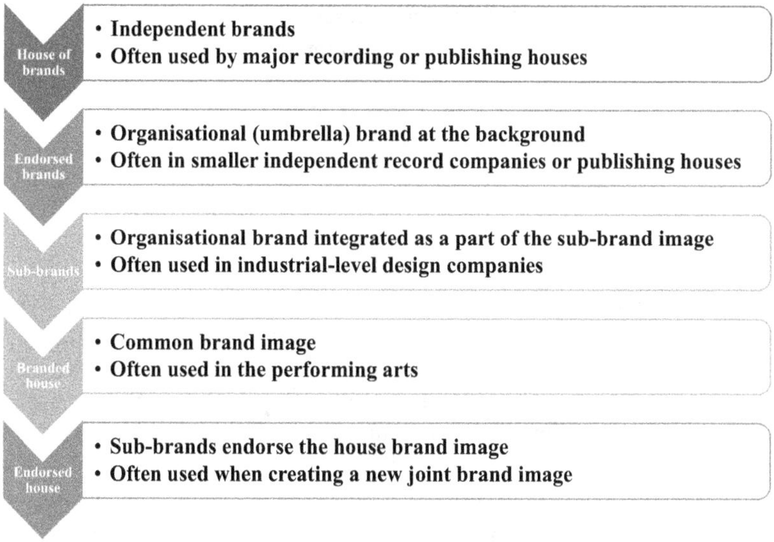

Figure 6.2 Brand architecture strategies and examples of cultural fields

Source: Adapted from Aaker & Joachimsthaler, (2000a, 2000b); Jyrämä et al. (2015).

Brand architecture strategy helps managers make sense of the brand portfolio. In each of the strategies, the relationship between the brands is looked at through the power or dominance dimensions, questioning if there is one brand dominating all the others, not a main brand with shared dominance, or if each of the individual (product) brands builds its own image, with shared dominance.

6.5 Brand alliances

The forming of brand alliances is yet another way to look at joint branding. Brand alliances are created to support geographical extensions and enhance the speed of market entry. Synergy offers many benefits and researching new customer groups and joining up with existing brands allows for low investment when entering new markets; however, there might be less control regarding the entry and brand management decisions (Barwise & Robertson, 1992).

Brand alliances can take various forms. One example that comes readily to mind is the combining of two brands through their ingredients, such as cookies in ice cream. In addition, brand alliances may take the form of joint promotion, in which two brands are presented in one advertisement, for instance a concert combined with a restaurant meal. Dual branding is a type of brand alliance in which two brands are located in the same space. This is familiar in the context of fast-food restaurants but is also strategically used by other types of restaurants as well as hotels. In the context of cultural joint ventures, the cultural organisations share joint space, and the integrating brand or alliance is built through the space (see more forthcoming, e.g., the Helsinki Music Centre case) (see also more discussion in Levin, 2002; Washburn et al., 2004).

The benefits of brand alliances are multiple and pairing up brand images can increase the positive perceptions of customers. Connecting two familiar brands builds trust and reduces the need to search for information on a new product (Washburn et al., 2004). Especially when the product or service is difficult to evaluate, brand alliances may enhance their acceptability. This is particularly important in the field of culture, in which the quality of a service or product is often hard to evaluate. Brand alliance builds on the familiarity of the joined brands to attain benefits such as larger customer groups and faster access to new markets. However, the existing studies raise important questions, such as: does the higher-image brand risk losing its quality image if it joins with a lesser brand? Does a complementary or similar brand alliance bring better benefits? The brand alliance needs to be carefully evaluated as, if unsuccessful, it might bring down both brands; yet, when successful, it adds brand equity and a greater reach of customers for both (see Levin & Levin, 2000; Ruiliang & Cao, 2017; Washburn et al., 2004; Yan & Cao, 2017).

The ways brand portfolio and brand architecture are focused on company/organisation-centred views have received criticism (e.g., Åsberg, 2018; Leitch & Richardson, 2003). Åsberg (2018) points out that it is the customers who fill in the gaps in company portfolios by identifying the brands from their partners or competitors to add while also increasing the demand for the product/service at hand in general. Leitch and Richardson (2003) propose a web of brands to complement the brand portfolio and brand architecture perspectives in which the focus is on the brand relationships beyond company/organisational borders. This approach adds insight when looking at brand relationships and strategies, especially in the joint-venture context. In addition, Åsberg and Uggla (2019) argue that the traditional brand-architecture model does not capture the complexity and multitude of possibilities of brand architecture, and they propose a different model that allows for a change in perception, from (simple) categorisation to multidimensional: for example, in terms of structure, from mono-brand to multi-brand, and in relation to orientation, from closed to open. This allows organisations to reflect on a multitude of choices for brand architecture, rather than be limited to choosing from established categorisations. They also emphasise the role of a third (or additional) partner or brand to further enhance the brand perception by customers. In each of the models, the relationship between brands is looked at through their power relationship or dominance, questioning whether there is one brand that dominates the others, not a dominant brand with shared dominance, or if the individual (product) brands are building their own image, thus sharing dominance.

Similarly, Leitch and Richardson (2003) point out how brands exist in networks or webs and highlight the importance of brand relationships. They propose that branding in the context of multiple organisational identities should have as its starting point branding around values, through which customers identify multiple meanings, thus allowing for multiple identity formations that build multiple relationships towards joint goals. Building from the networked perspective, the brand architecture approach captures more complex, yet common, branding situations. Thus, branding needs to consider not only the joint brands but also the effects of the organisation's parent company and the competing brands. We will return to the role of other partners in Part III, especially noting the roles of parent companies.

Next, we explore the previously mentioned approaches on joining brands, brand alliances, brand portfolios, and brand architecture strategies in relation to different cases of cultural joint ventures.

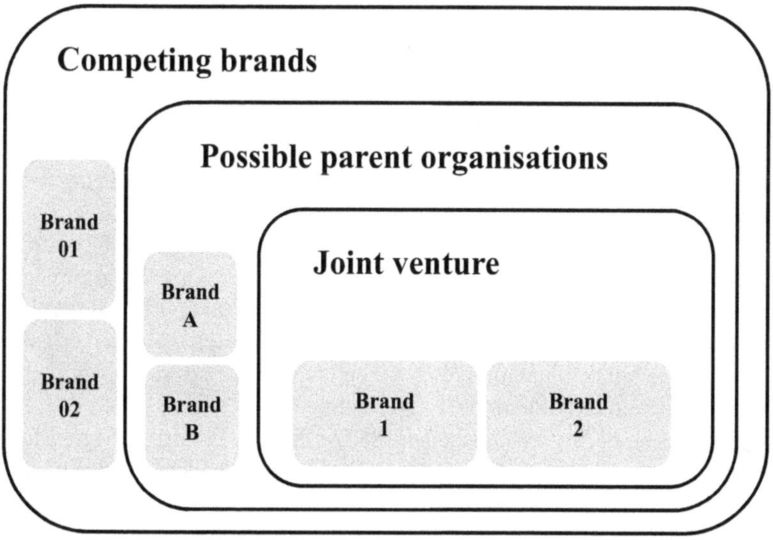

Figure 6.3 Composition of brand architecture in cultural joint ventures

7 Cases and managerial implications

7.1. Case 1: Helsinki Music Centre, Helsinki, Finland

Helsinki Music Centre (HMC) unites three existing and long-standing brands into a joint entity. These are the Helsinki Philharmonic Orchestra (HPO), the Finnish Radio Symphony Orchestra (FRSO), and the Sibelius Academy (SA), which is the leading music university in Finland. This analysis of their brand images and relationships is based on research conducted prior to the opening of the new Helsinki Music Centre and is aimed at understanding each organisation's brand image, i.e., perceptions of their customers, at the starting point of the new venture (the case is based on Mäkinen, 2012; for a more detailed analysis, see Mäkinen, 2012, and Jyrämä et al., 2015).

The Finnish Radio Symphony Orchestra (FRSO) (established in 1927) is the orchestra of the Finnish Broadcasting Company (Yle). Its mission is to produce and promote Finnish musical culture. The orchestra primarily gives concerts at the Helsinki Music Centre. Its main funding comes from television-licence fees from the Finnish population (https://yle.fi/aihe/artikkeli/2014/06/23/finnish-radio-symphony-orchestra; https://en.wikipedia.org/wiki/Finnish_Radio_Symphony_Orchestra).

The Helsinki Philharmonic Orchestra's (established in 1883) aim is "to give the people of Helsinki a chance to hear great musical masterpieces at a series of weekly concerts." The HPO is governed as a bureau of the Helsinki City Council. Its primary concert venue is the Helsinki Music Centre (https://helsinginkaupunginorkesteri.fi/en/orchestra; https://en.wikipedia.org/wiki/Helsinki_Philharmonic_Orchestra).

Sibelius Academy (established in 1882) is the only Finnish university that offers postgraduate degrees in music. With 1,500 students and 500 teachers, it is one of the largest music academies in Europe. Since 2013, the Sibelius Academy has been part of the University of the Arts Helsinki together with the Theatre Academy and the Academy of Fine Arts (www.uniarts.fi/en/units/sibelius-academy/; https://en.wikipedia.org/wiki/Sibelius_Academy).

DOI: 10.4324/9780429273919-9

The three organisational brands and the brand image of the Helsinki Music Centre were analysed in order to understand the respective organisational brand images at the early stages of their joint venture after their relocation to a joint space at the Helsinki Music Centre.

Managerial challenge

The managerial challenge we were interested in was how to create a brand image for a new joint venture.

Managerial responses

To understand the brand relationships of a new joint venture, one needs to understand the current brand images of the joining brands—for example, what kinds of brand personalities the joining organisations have, and how the current customers identify themselves to the existing brands in terms of brand loyalty. The new joint venture needs to provide ways for its customers to evaluate and build a relationship with the new joint venture. For example, what are the special values and benefits it wishes to offer to them in the future, and what images and expectations does it wish to convey through its brands (Basu, 2006; Mäkinen, 2012)?

In the case of the Helsinki Music Centre, in evaluating the existing brands to better understand the possible branding strategies for the joint venture, the organisational brand images were analysed according to their: 1) brand loyalty, 2) brand attitude, 3) brand associations and perceived quality, 4) behavioural expectations, and 5) brand personality. These dimensions are illustrated in the following figure.

Brand-image dimensions

The results of the analysis (factor analysis) revealed five underlying dimensions that explain the brand image and brand-image dimensions that are perceived by the respondents, the dimensions of brand image in this context.

1. Positive attitude towards the new joint brand contained the most variables of the new identified dimensions. The main items in this dimension represent the brand-attitude dimension of brand image from the previous research, with some explanations of brand associations and perceived quality, behavioural expectations, and loyalty dimensions in this factor. All of the variables reflect highly positive attitudes and associations towards the new joint brand.

2. Strong brand loyalty towards the existing brands connects strongly to the brand-loyalty dimension of brand image except for one item, the behavioural-expectations dimension.

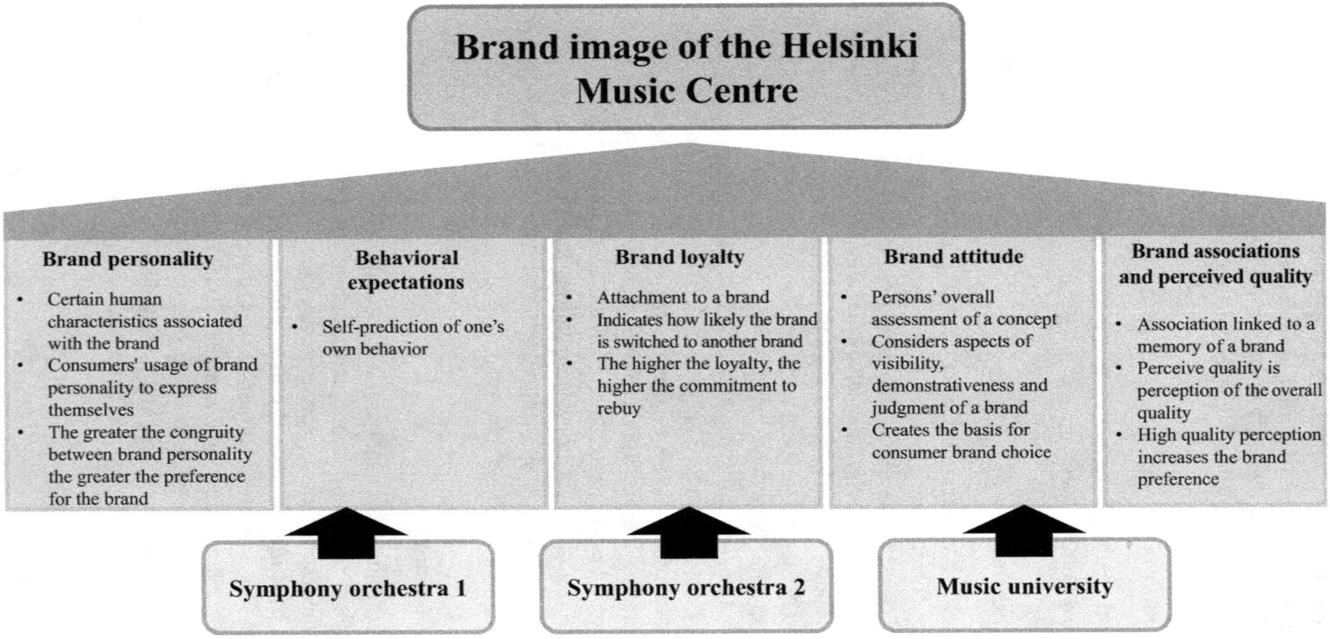
Brand image of the Helsinki Music Centre
Brand personality
Certain human characteristics associated with the brand
Consumers' usage of brand personality to express themselves
The greater the congruity between brand personality the greater the preference for the brand
Behavioral expectations
Self-prediction of one's own behavior
Brand loyalty
Attachment to a brand
Indicates how likely the brand is switched to another brand
The higher the loyalty, the higher the commitment to rebuy
Brand attitude
Persons' overall assessment of a concept
Considers aspects of visibility, demonstrativeness and judgment of a brand
Creates the basis for consumer brand choice
Brand associations and perceived quality
Association linked to a memory of a brand
Perceive quality is perception of the overall quality
High quality perception increases the brand preference
Symphony orchestra 1
Symphony orchestra 2
Music university

Figure 7.1 Construction of the brand image of Helsinki Music Centre

Source: Adapted from Mäkinen (2012).

3. Positive behavioural expectations regarding the new joint brand include items mainly from the explanations of behavioural expectations and loyalty. Additionally, the loyalty variables indicate behavioural expectations. This dimension clearly shows positive behavioural expectations towards the new joint brand. It captures the loyalty to existing brands as well as the expectations of emerging consumers of the new joint brand.

4. Recognition of visual and functional attributes of the new joint brand builds on brand associations and the perceived quality dimension of the brand image for the new joint brand.

5. Low-quality expectations and negative associations towards the new joint brand represent brand associations and the perceived quality dimension of the brand image. All items in this dimension indicate low-perceived quality expectations and negative associations towards the new joint brand.

Moreover, the customers can be grouped into the following segments using the identified brand-image dimensions (cluster analysis).

The segment that includes **loyal customers of the existing brands** consists of the loyal customers of each of the existing arts organisations. Customers were seen as the stakeholders who plan to visit the concerts of the organisations. They have strong brand loyalty towards the existing brands. Moreover, they are positive towards the new joint brand, as they do not have low expectations of quality or negative associations towards it. This segment (cluster) was the largest.

People with **positive attitudes towards the new joint brand** were identified as one segment which consists of respondents who are enthusiastic about the new joint brand. They do not have strong brand loyalty towards the existing brands. Instead, they have positive behavioural expectations regarding the new joint brand. This segment (cluster) was the second largest.

People with **negative attitudes** have low expectations of quality and negative associations towards the new joint brand. They do not have positive attitudes towards the existing brands. In the analysis, this was the smallest group (cluster).

Hence, at the beginning of the joint venture, most customers were loyal customers of the existing brands, which is not surprising. These loyalties translated into positive feelings towards the start of the new brand of the joint venture. However, having a small group of customers with negative attitudes is somewhat surprising as the survey was conducted among the current customers of the three organisations.

The brand-personality dimension of brand image was analysed separately (central tendency analysis). The brand personalities of each of the brands, HMC, FRSO, and HPO, were analysed by asking the respondents

Table 7.1 Brand personalities perceived by the customers of cultural joint ventures

Adjective	*FRSO*	*HPO*	*SIBA*	*HMC*
Approachable, versatile, experiential, and international	high	somewhat	less approachable	rather high
Attractive	high	less	less	high
Forerunner	higher	somewhat	higher	higher
Interactive and down-to-earth	somewhat	somewhat	somewhat	somewhat
Wholesome and happy	somewhat	somewhat	somewhat	somewhat
Family-oriented	rather low	rather low	rather low	rather low
Sincere, emotional, genuine, and friendly	high	somewhat	somewhat	low
Daring, imaginative	highest	somewhat	high	somewhat
Modern	somewhat	somewhat	somewhat	highest
Exciting and unique	somewhat	a bit less	somewhat	somewhat
Trustworthy	high	high	somewhat	somewhat
Upper-class	low	low	low	low

to evaluate the brand on each adjective from the brand personality measurement (Aaker, 1997). The results showed that the brand personalities were rather similar, and only minor differences could be detected. It is noteworthy to point out that most respondents were loyal customers of FRSO, hence, the results were most likely somewhat biased. The brand personality often reflected the customer's own personality, as part of the brand relationship.

The table below summarises the main results of the brand personalities as perceived by the customers.

To summarise, HPO was considered less of a forerunner, daring, or modern, but more trustworthy and approachable. This fits with the tradition of the orchestra, as HPO has the deepest roots of all the organisations. Founded in 1883, it is the oldest philharmonic orchestra in the Nordic countries. FRSO, on the other hand, emphasises its goal of enhancing Finnish musical culture, both nationally and internationally, and it has been granted international awards that match its personality traits, such as international, versatile, and successful. Sibelius Academy, the only high-quality music university in Finland, is seen as less approachable, as reflected in the difficulty of gaining entrance to study at the institution. The brand personality traits for the HMC were similar to the organisational brands but were seen as more modern, which might reflect its entry to the field. It is noteworthy to point out that it was difficult to evaluate the HMC brand because the customers had not yet experienced the new joint-venture brand. Hence, it seemed that the brand personality of the HMC was constructed through the brand personalities of the existing brands. Nevertheless, all the initial brands were close to each other, with only minor differences.

How then can we use our knowledge and understanding of brand-image dimension and customer segments in our management of the brand image of the new joint venture?

The analysis of the joining brand images with the first perceptions of the new joint brand HMC provides insight for managers to reflect on what kinds of brand portfolio or brand architecture they could create. It is important to notice that at this point of a joint venture, early in its creation, the existing brand images can be seen as endorsing the new joint-brand image. In this process, questions naturally arise about what kind of image they are building, what are the common features, and what seem to be the differences.

In the case of HMC, the joining brand images have several storing points in common. When looking at the brand personality analysis, the differences seem rather subtle and build towards a somewhat common personality for the new joint venture as well. On the other hand, the brand loyalty is connected to the individual organisational brands, i.e., customers have a strong relationship with one of the current brand images that belongs to the brand community of the initial organisations. The management then needs to reflect on whether to promote strong individual organisation brands as its brand portfolio strategy in the future, i.e., house of brand or brand architecture strategy, or to try to manage the brand images towards other choices. What might be the benefits and disadvantages of these potential future choices?

In the case of the HMC, the individual organisational brands have been kept independent, with each organisation maintaining its own brand, with its loyal customers. Even now, the HMC management seems to follow the house of brands or the endorsed house brand architecture strategy. This allows the joining organisations to keep their independence, as in this case, the differences are so subtle that trying to merge the brands into one might result in a situation in which one of the organisations becomes obsolete. Hence, the brand-image differences, even though subtle, have been emphasised.

However, on the other hand, the HMC has gained, through endorsing the organisational brands, its own brand image. It has built on the brand images of the organisational brands, reflecting their personalities, yet developed its own image that is reflected in the brand dimensions, such as visuality and functionality. The HMC and its brand is, on the one hand, responsible for the functional side of the actual product, i.e., the concert visits, and, on the other hand, for creating the visual atmosphere of the event, through the visual image of the building, its brand, and the surroundings. It also offers a joint platform for marketing communication, including its visual and functional image.

7.2 Case 2: Concertgebouw, Amsterdam, Netherlands

In 1881, six citizens in Amsterdam came together to create a provisional committee aiming to build a concert hall. The concert hall was built in five years, but due to some difficulties with funders and municipalities, it was not opened until 1888. The concert hall was given the name "the Concertgebouw" and its unparalleled acoustics were highly praised nationally and internationally. The Concertgebouw has three different halls: the Main Hall (1,974 seats), the Recital Hall (437 seats), and the recently opened Choir Hall (150 seats). The mission of the Concertgebouw is to offer as many people as possible the opportunity to experience the magnificent power of music that benefits from the unique qualities of the Concertgebouw (for a more detailed analysis of the case, please see Jyrämä & Johansson, 2017).

The Concertgebouw organises over 900 events per year, of which 80% are concerts. Approximately 700,000 visitors visit the concert hall a year. The Concertgebouw has a house orchestra, the Royal Concertgebouw Orchestra, which has been voted the best orchestra in the world. Ever since its opening in 1888, the Concertgebouw has been a privately owned and mainly privately financed company, with only about 5% of its revenues governmentally subsidised. The revenues of the Concertgebouw come from ticket sales (30%), rentals (22%), hospitality (20%), fundraising and sponsorship (20%), and other sources (8%, incl. 5% from the municipality).

The Concertgebouw in Amsterdam stages its own productions as well as hosts both its "own" named music ensembles, such as Royal Concertgebouw Orchestra, as well as the concerts of the Netherland National Philharmonic Orchestra. The Concertgebouw provides programming, marketing, and facility management, as well as, for example, initiatives for audience development and social responsibility.

Managerial challenge

The managerial challenge related to the brand images was how and why to maintain a strong house brand image in the changing lifestyles that affect a cultural joint venture.

Managerial response

In the case of the Concertgebouw, its long history and the house orchestra's fame contribute to the strong house-brand image. The Concertgebouw has decided on a branded house strategy and, in addition to the hosted ensembles, it selects its other programmes carefully to fit the brand image and the characteristics of the concert hall, namely its outstanding acoustics. The

Concertgebouw's own production of additional special events and concerts contributes to the joint-brand image. On the one hand, the strong brand image has created loyal customers and interest among visitors and tourists, yet keeping its loyal customers while building interest for the long term with emerging generations is the main challenge for the Concertgebouw. The management must consider how to maintain its strong brand identification with all the ensembles, a diminishing number of loyal customers, and an ever-growing number of unknown customers, who seem to decide to attend a concert on the same day as the event. Thus, the Concertgebouw is facing the issue of lifestyle changes, from regular concertgoers to last-minute decision-makers.

The Concertgebouw has responded to the changing lifestyle issue by facilitating the access and ease of concert visits. It collaborates, for example, with local public transport to ensure low costs and easy access to the venue.

Brand architecture strategy

The brand architecture strategy of the Concertgebouw can be categorised as a branded house. The brand identity of the Concertgebouw builds strongly on its long history and the building itself; it is strongly connected to classical and acoustic music, the quality of which is at the core of its brand identity, strengthened by its own productions as well as its own music ensembles. The brand image of the Concertgebouw connects to the advancement of musical appreciation, not only through the ensembles but through the Concertgebouw organisation itself. Hence, it can be categorised as a branded house brand architecture strategy, even if it hosts other independent brands, such as the Netherland National Philharmonic Orchestra.

Organisational structure and culture—identifying organisational identity

The Concertgebouw in Amsterdam stages its own productions and hosts both its own named music ensembles, such as Royal Concertgebouw Orchestra, as well as regular concerts of the Netherland National Philharmonic Orchestra. In the context of the Concertgebouw, programming and activities knowledge is shared in terms of future performances, marketing, and facility management, as well as, for example, initiatives for audience development and social responsibility. We propose that the Concertgebouw's organisational structure is a network-based one, in which the sharing of knowledge, joint activities, facilities, and marketing support its overall artistic offerings.

Perceived brand identity and co-branding strategy

Even though the brand identity of the Concertgebouw builds strongly on its long history and the building itself, it is strongly connected to classical and acoustic music, the quality of which is at the core of its brand identity. This music at its core is strengthened by its own productions as well as its own music ensembles. This artistic/musical identity is also strengthened by, for example, a resident-composer programme that links the Concertgebouw with the advancement of music, not only through the ensembles, but through the Concertgebouw organisation itself. We suggest that the Concertgebouw is categorised as a branded house, although this might be too strong a categorisation with respect to the visiting organisations, such as the Netherland National Philharmonic Orchestra.

7.3 Case 3: Auckland Live, Auckland, New Zealand

Auckland Live is New Zealand's largest hub of performing-arts venues, which opened in 1990. Auckland Live describes itself as an arts and entertainment organisation aiming to be recognised as a creative hub and catalyst for new ideas. It provides a range of different arts and entertainment opportunities, presenting live arts events at a number of venues across Auckland and providing support to the arts and creative sector, as well as opportunities for people to engage with the arts. Auckland Live joins Auckland and New Zealand's treasured national and regional arts companies, and their several festivals (for a more detailed analysis of the case, see Jyrämä & Johansson, 2017).

At the time of the study, Auckland Live hosted nine different arts organisations: New Zealand Symphony Orchestra, New Zealand Opera, Chamber Music Auckland, Royal New Zealand Ballet, Auckland Philharmonia Orchestra, Auckland Arts Festival, New Zealand International Comedy Festival, New Zealand International Film Festival, and Auckland Writers Festival. Auckland Live's responsibility was to ensure that all venues (at the time of the study, there were eight venues) provided a suitable setting for events, and it supported each organisation's campaigns with marketing insights and local knowledge on customers. Each location has an independent image; for example, in February 2016, the Auckland Philharmonia Orchestra relocated its operations to the Auckland Town Hall, bringing the administration and musicians under the one roof of their performance home.

The organisational structure of Auckland Live consists of independent host organisations to which Auckland Live provides facility, marketing, and production services. Auckland Live is part of the regional organisation as well. It has a rather siloed organisational structure, with each ensemble being independent and mainly sharing the facilities and marketing activities. It seems that Auckland Live operates both with respect to the regional organisation and the arts organisations that belong to it. This refers to a rather siloed organisational structure, with each ensemble being independent and mainly sharing facilities and marketing activities.

Managerial challenge

The managerial challenge we were interested in was how to maintain connectedness among the partnering organisations, considering their independent brand images.

Managerial response

Auckland Live has had two major brand changes. The organisation originated from the Aotea Centre, a performing-arts venue that was built around a municipal facility from 1990 to 1997. In 1997, the EDGE brand was created as other venues were added to the organisation, such as Auckland Town Hall. In 2010, EDGE was taken under the regional facilities when Auckland Council was formed. Thus, the emphasis has remained on the facility management and maintenance of the premises. In 2014, the current brand name Auckland Live was adopted in the desire to build stronger jointly shared marketing activities and to build an umbrella brand depicting a strong art and entertainment identity. However, the brand identity seems to be a house of brands, in which each of the organisations has its own strong brand. This indicates that Auckland Live has not become an integral part of their respective identities.

References

Aaker, D. A. (1991). *Managing brand equity*. New York: The Free Press.

Aaker, D. A. (1996). *Building strong brands*. New York: The Free Press.

Aaker, D. A., & Joachimsthaler, E. (2000a). *Brand leadership*. New York: The Free Press.

Aaker, D. A., & Joachimsthaler, E. (2000b). The brand relationship spectrum: The key to the brand architecture challenge. *California Management Review*, *42*(4), 8–23.

Aaker, J. L. (1997). Dimensions of brand personality. *Journal of Marketing Research*, *34*(3), 347–356.

Anholt, S. (2009). Should place brands be simple? *Place Branding and Public Diplomacy*, *5*(2), 91–96.

Åsberg, P. (2018). A dualistic view of brand portfolios: The company's versus the customers' view. *Journal of Consumer Marketing, 24*(6), 610–620.

Åsberg, P., & Uggla, H. (2019). Introducing multi-dimensional brand architecture: Taking structure, market orientation and stakeholder alignment into account. *Journal of Brand Management*, *26*, 483–496.

Baker, M. J., & Balmer, J. M. (1997). Visual identity: Trappings or substance? *European Journal of Marketing, 31*(5/6), 366–382.

Balmer, J. M. T. (1995). Corporate branding and connoisseurship. *Journal of General Management, 21*(1), 24–46.

Balmer, J. M. T. (2001). Corporate identity, corporate branding and corporate marketing. Seeing through the fog. *European Journal of Marketing, 35*(3/4), 248–291.

Barwise, P., & Robertson, T. (1992). Brand portfolios. *European Management Journal, 10*(3), 277–285.

Basu, K. (2006). Merging brands after mergers. *California Management Review, 48*(4), 28–40.

Batra, R., Aaron, A., & Bagozzi, R. P. (2012). Brand love. *Journal of Marketing, 76*(2), 1–16.

Brunner, C., & Baum, M. (2020). The impact of brand portfolios on organizational attractiveness. *Journal of Business Research, 106*, 182–195.

Camarero, C., Garrido, M. J., & Vicente, E. (2010). Components of art exhibition brand equity for internal and external visitors. *Tourism Management, 31*(4), 495–504.

Camarero, C., Garrido, M. J., & Vicente, E. (2011). How cultural organizations' size and funding influence innovation and performance: The case of museums. *Journal of Cultural Economics, 35*(4), 247–266.

Carroll, B. A., & Ahuvia, A. C. (2006). Some antecedents and outcomes of brand love. *Marketing Letters, 17*(2), 79–89.

Chaudhuri, A., & Holbrook, M. B. (2001). The chain of effects from brand trust and brand affect to brand performance: The role of brand loyalty. *The Journal of Marketing, 65*, 81–93.

Colbert, F. (2009). *Beyond branding: Contemporary marketing challenges for arts organizations*. Geelong: Deakin University.

Colbert, F., & St-James, Y. (2014). Research in arts marketing: Evolution and future directions. *Psychology & Marketing, 31*(8), 566–575.

d'Astous, A., Colbert, F., & Fournier, M. (2007). An experimental investigation of the use of brand extension and co-branding strategies in the arts. *Journal of Services Marketing, 21*(4), 231–240.

del Barrio-García, S., & Prados-Peña, M. (2019). Do brand authenticity and brand credibility facilitate brand equity? The case of heritage destination brand extension. *Journal of Destination Marketing & Management, 13*, 10–23.

Gabrielli, V., & Baghi, I. (2020). Unveiling the corporate brand: The role of portfolio composition. *Journal of Consumer Marketing, 37*(3), 279–290.

Gombault, A., & Selles, D. (2018). Louvre Abu Dhabi: A radical innovation, but what future for French cultural influence? *International Journal of Arts Management, 20*(3), 83–94.

Harish, R. (2008). The concept and origin of brand architecture: A comprehensive literature survey. *ICFAI Journal of Brand Management*, 5(4), 51–62.

He, H., & Li, Y. (2010). CSR and service brand: The mediating effect of brand identification and moderating effect of service quality. *Journal of Business Ethics, 100*(4), 673–688.

Hieke, S. (2010). Effects of counterfeits on the image of luxury brands: An empirical study from the customer perspective. *Journal of Brand Management, 18*(2), 159–173.

Hsieh, M.-H., Shan-Ling, P., & Setiono, R. (2004). Product-, corporate-, and country-image dimensions and purchase behavior: A multicountry analysis. *Journal of the Academy of Marketing Science*, *32*(3), 251–270.

Janonis, V., Dovalienė, A., & Virvilaitė, R. (2007). Relationship of brand identity and image. *Engineering Economics*, *51*(1), 69–79.

Johansson, T., & Jyrämä, A. (2016). Network of Organizational Identities in the Formation of a Cultural Joint Venture: A Case Study of the Helsinki Music Centre. *International Journal of Arts Management*, 67–78.

Jyrämä, A. (2017). Branding the arts—Some perspectives. In T. Johansson & M. Luonila (Eds.), *Making sense of arts management: Research, cases and practices*. Sibelius Academy Publications 11. Helsinki: Unigrafia.

Jyrämä, A., & Johansson, T. (2017, July). Co-branding an identity—International comparison of music centres. In *Proceedings of AIMAC 2017*, Peking.

Jyrämä, A., Kajalo, S., Johansson, T., & Mäkinen, A. (2015). Brand image of merging brands: An empirical analysis of the merge of two orchestras and a music university. *Journal of Art Management, Law and Society*, *45*(3), 193–206.

Kapferer, J.-N. (2004). *New strategic brand management. Creating and sustaining brand equity long term* (3rd ed.). London and Sterling, VA: Kogan Page.

Keller, K. L. (1993). Conceptualizing, measuring, and managing customer-based brand equity. *Journal of Marketing*, *57*(1), 1–22.

Keller, K. L. (2012). Economic and behavioral perspectives on brand extensions. *Marketing Science*, *31*(5), 772–776.

Keller, K. L., & Lehmann, D. D. (2006). Brands and branding: Research findings and future priorities. *Marketing Science*, *25*(6), 740–759.

Kim, M., Tang, C. H., & Roehl, W. S. (2018). The effect of hotel's dual-branding on willingness-to-pay and booking intention: A luxury/upper-upscale combination. *Journal of Revenue Pricing Management*, *17*, 256–275.

King, S. (1991). Brand-building in the 1990s. *Journal of Consumer Marketing*, *8*(4), 43–52.

Kotler, P., & Scheff, J. (1997). *Standing room only: Strategies for marketing the performing arts*. Harvard Business School Press.

Lee, J. S. (1995). Role of attitude toward brand advertising on consumer perception of a brand extension. *Advances in Consumer Research, 22*, 116–122.

Leijerholt, U., Chapleo, C., & O'Sullivan, H. (2019). A brand within a brand: An integrated understanding of internal brand management and brand architecture in the public sector. *Journal of Brand Management*, *26*, 277–290.

Leitch, S., & Richardson, N. (2003). Corporate branding in the new economy. *European Journal of Marketing*, *37*(7/8), 1065–1079.

Levin, A. M. (2002). Contrast and assimilation processes in consumers' evaluations of dual brands. *Journal of Business and Psychology*, *17*, 145–154.

Levin, I. P., & Levin, A. M. (2000). Modeling the role of brand alliances in the assimilation of product evaluations. *Journal of Consumer Psychology*, *9*(1), 43–52.

Lindroos, S., Nyman, G., & Lindroos, K. (2005). *Kirkas Brandi. Miten suomalainen tuote erottuu, lisää arvoaan ja perustelee hintansa*. Helsinki: WSOY.

Mäkinen, A. (2012). *Brand image as an indicator of brand relationships and architecture in Helsinki Music Centre—Case study of three merging brands: Helsinki*

Philharmonic Orchestra, Finnish Radio Symphony Orchestra and Sibelius Academy. Master thesis, Aalto University, School of Business.

Marin, L., & Ruiz, S. (2006). I need you too! Corporate identity attractiveness for consumers and the role of social responsibility. *Journal of Business Ethics*, *71*(3), 245–260.

Marin, L., Ruiz, S., & Rubio, A. (2008). The role of identity salience in the effects of corporate social responsibility on consumer behavior. *Journal of Business Ethics*, *84*(1), 65–78.

Mazodier, M., & Merunka, D. (2012). Achieving brand loyalty through sponsorship: The role of fit and self-congruity. *Journal of the Academy of Marketing Science*, *40*(6), 807–820.

Morgan, N. A., & Rego, L. L. (2009). Brand portfolio strategy and firm performance. *Journal of Marketing*, *73*(1), 59–74.

Oliver, R. L. (1999). Whence consumer loyalty? *Journal of Marketing*, *63*(4), 33–44.

Park, W. C., Jaworski, B. J., & Maclnnis, D. J. (1986). Strategic brand concept-image management. *Journal of Marketing*, *50*(4), 135–145.

Peter, P. J., & Olson, J. C. (2005). *Consumer behavior & marketing strategy* (7th ed.). New York: McGraw-Hill Irwin.

Plaza, B. (2008). On some challenges and conditions for the Guggenheim Museum Bilbao to be an effective economic re-activator. *International Journal of Urban and Regional Research*, *32*(2), 506–517.

Punniyamoorthy, M., & Prasanna Mohan Raj, M. (2007). An empirical model for brand loyalty measurement. *Journal of Targeting, Measurement and Analysis for Marketing*, *15*(4), 222–233.

Pusa, S., & Uusitalo, L. (2014). Creating brand identity in art museums: A case study. *International Journal of Arts Management*, *17*(1), 18.

Ritvala, T., Granqvist, N., & Piekkari, R. (2021). A processual view of organizational stigmatization in foreign market entry: The failure of Guggenheim Helsinki. *Journal of International Business Studies*, *52*(2), 282–305.

Ruiliang, Y., & Cao, Z. (2017). Is brand alliance always beneficial to firms? *Journal of Retailing and Consumer Services*, *34*, 193–200.

Scheff, J., & Kotler, P. (1996). Crisis in the arts: The marketing response. *California Management Review*, *39*(1), 28.

Spry, L., Foster, C., Pich, C., & Peart, S. (2020). Managing higher education brands with an emerging brand architecture: The role of shared values and competing brand identities. *Journal of Strategic Marketing*, *28*(4), 336–349.

Swanson, S. R., & Davis, J. C. (2006). Arts patronage: A social identity perspective. *Journal of Marketing Theory and Practice*, *14*(2), 125–138.

Venable, B. T., Rose, G. M., Bush, W. D., & Gilbert, F. D. (2005). The role of brand personality in charitable giving: An assessment and validation. *Journal of the Academy of Marketing Science*, *33*(3), 295–312.

Washburn, J. H., Till, B. D., & Priluck, R. (2004). Brand alliance and customer-based brand-equity effects. *Psychology & Marketing*, *21*(7), 487–508.

Yan, R., & Cao, Z. (2017). Is brand alliance always beneficial to firms? *Journal of Retailing and Consumer Services*, *34*, 193–200.

Part III

Bridging the multiple identities and images of cultural joint ventures

Part III bridges the two previous parts and considers how the identity-image view can be combined to facilitate an alignment of the management practices of cultural joint ventures. Chapter 8 presents approaches to enable a better understanding of the joint venture and its collaborating organisations, including the role of organisational structures and practices in crossing boundaries and building a shared understanding of organisational identities and brands. This is followed by a discussion of values and art as the core on which the identity-image view of a joint venture is built. This chapter discusses different perceptions of the arts and artistic quality in the context of cultural joint ventures, which affects the way organisational members make sense of their own organisation and its brand. Furthermore, we discuss how the organisational members may perceive and identify with the other organisations and brands within the same joint venture. Part III concludes with short cases to provide concrete examples of the processes involved in building an identity-image view of a cultural joint venture.

DOI: 10.4324/9780429273919-10

8 Components of an identity-image view of cultural joint ventures

In joint ventures, as discussed earlier, a new joint organisational identity and brand image(s) are inevitably created when the two existing ones are combined. In previous literature, the process of strategically building a new joint identity and brand image has been discussed (see chapter 2), as well as how the new identity and brand images emerge through organisational practice (see De Chernatony, 1999). When looking at both avenues, we note that joint identity and brand image are built through knowledge sharing, organisational structure, and culture, which influences the ability to support and encourage joint practices (see Johansson & Jyrämä, 2016; Kauppila et al., 2011).

These underlying elements, organisational structure, culture, and adopted practice(s), can be both barriers to and enablers of change, as well as shared identity and brand image (e.g., Zollo & Winter, 2002). In addition, the values inherent in organisational culture have been found to affect art organisations, with art playing and occupying a special role (see Jyrämä & Äyväri, 2010). Hence, the role of organisational culture as enabling or inhibiting shared knowledge and shared activities can be seen as contributing to a joint identity and brand image. Its role is vital for all kinds of arts organisations, but especially in the case of joint ventures. In addition, Beamish and Lupton (2009) identified some key issues affecting the management of joint ventures. We follow the themes proposed in their nominal article, namely knowledge management and governance, in our joint venture analysis.

As mentioned above, the organisational structure, culture, and practice have been found to influence the way in which knowledge is shared and how practices are created in organisations, in particular in joint ventures in which two existing organisational structures, cultures, and practices have been combined. These key concepts are intertwined and mutually influencing. Next, we introduce each of them and discuss their interconnectedness.

DOI: 10.4324/9780429273919-11

8.1 Organisational structure

Organisational structure tackles topics such as centralisation or decentralisation in decision-making; questions related to the organisation of functional departments and their connectedness; and the role of managers, middle managers, and employees, which often relate to questions of power and hierarchies.

Discussions of organisational structure often have as a starting point Weber's (1994) classical elaboration on bureaucracy and other forms of governance. Organisational structures guide how an organisation is led and what kinds of internal divisions and decision paths it has (e.g., Hsu et al., 1983). Early on, organisational structure was often analysed vis-à-vis bureaucracy, relating its structure either to bureaucratic or other forms of structure, such as networked or community-based. In a very simplified manner, we can state that organisational structure looks at how an organisation is divided into functions, how the functions communicate or not, and how decisions are made within the internal structure of an organisation. Questions about the allocation of authority, the division of power into centralised or decentralised forms, and the ways different departments and functions cooperate are in focus. For example, are the functions performed in silos or are joint practices in place via internal networks or communities?

The organisational structure is usually explicitly created by defining power relationships, hierarchical levels, and dividing the operational functions into departments. However, the underlying variables behind these choices can be varied. Some of the identified determinants guiding these decisions are the size of the organisation, the perceived costs of the organisational structure or its change, the support of operations by technology, and traditions and trends (see Colombo & Delmastro, 2002). The contextual variables that influence the structural characteristics of an organisation and their relationships have been widely discussed (e.g., Colombo & Delmastro, 2002). The variables or determinants analysed have included, among others, the organisation's size, the role of technology, the relationships within the organisational context, and the organisational complexity. These variables have been found to affect the organisational structure, namely decisions about the centralisation or decentralisation of authority, hierarchical layers or line management of the workflow, standardisation or specialisation, and organisational control (see also Bäcklund et al., 2010). Some variables, such as the size and impact of technology, seem evident. For example, in micro-organisations, the hierarchical layers are fewer compared to large multinationals or organisations in which technological advancements, such as automation, occur (Colombo & Delmastro, 2002; Hsu et al., 1983; Pugh et al., 1969b).

The organisational complexity, i.e., the content of the organisational activity, plays a role, for example, in influencing the ways organisational departments are specialised or innovation projects are managed. Organisations with high levels of specialisation and expertise typically increase the degree of formalisation and decrease the concentration of decision-making on the top levels (Child, 1972, as cited in Hsu et al., 1983).

The organisation's dependency on other organisations, including the parent company, seems to lead to centralised decision-making and increased standardisation of procedures in, for example, human-relations management, yet it does not seem to affect either the formalisation or specialisation of activities (Pugh et al., 1969b). This finding plays an important role in the field of culture, as many of the cultural joint ventures studied had a "parent" company or organisation, such as a national broadcasting company or a city.

Next, we discuss the concept of organisational culture, which is inherently intertwined with the organisational structure, as this structure provides the "skeleton" for the ways in which organisational culture may emerge, develop, and adapt to the different phases of cultural joint venturing.

8.2 Organisational culture

Organisational culture has received plenty of attention in the management literature. It refers to the shared values, norms, ways of operating, and ways of behaving within an organisation. It can be observed, for example, in shared practices that build on shared values, shared rituals, and perceived heroes and symbols. It is socially constructed and hard to change. The organisational culture affects the ways an organisation interacts both on the inside but also with others (see Hofstede et al., 1990; Von Krogh et al., 2000). The organisational culture also affects the ways joining organisations act and manage in the context of joint ventures (see Shu et al., 2017), with an emphasis on the roles of trust (e.g., Gorondutse & Hilman, 2018), competition (e.g., Shu et al., 2017), national cultures (e.g., Pothukuchi et al., 2002), and underlying values (e.g., Johansson & Jyrämä, 2016).

Organisational culture has been found to affect the success of a joint venture, as organisations with a cultural fit usually find it easier to adopt joint actions and managerial practices. Therefore, organisations are advised to investigate the organisational culture of the potential partner prior to engaging in joint ventures (Fey & Beamish, 2001). Organisational cultures build on national cultures (see Hofstede et al., 1990), yet the national culture is only one element in organisational culture. It has been proposed that organisational culture affects the joint venture in more ways than just through the differences in national culture (Pothukuchi et al., 2002).

Organisational culture as a concept has been considered a "sister" concept to organisational identity as organisational identity builds on shared values, is affected by the organisational culture, and is shaped by managerial actions. In their nominal article, Hatch and Schultz (1997) elaborate on the conceptualisations of organisational identity, image, and organisation, by pointing out that organisational culture needs to be taken into account in the development and maintenance of organisational identity. Organisational culture creates a symbolic culture within which the various understandings of organisational identity are formed and the intentions to influence organisational images are formulated (Hatch & Schultz, 1997). Later, they continue their discussion on the connectedness of the concepts (e.g., Hatch & Schultz, 2002; Hatch & Zilber, 2012), which is an important aspect particularly in the context of cultural joint ventures.

The role of values cannot be ignored in the discussion of organisational culture, as the organisational identity or image that is reflected and manifested in the organisational culture and observed by stakeholders (image) is built on values (see Hatch, 1993; Hatch & Schultz, 1997). We will take a closer look at the core values for cultural joint ventures in other subchapters.

The role of trust is one of the characteristics mentioned by many scholars when analysing organisational culture and the ways organisations are managed (see Beamish & Lupton, 2009; Gorondutse & Hilman, 2018). For example, the level of freedom for employers, and the role of guidelines, rules, and control mechanisms all influence the organisational culture, and as discussed earlier, also are connected to the organisational structure hierarchies.

To summarise, a similarity in organisational cultures has been found to facilitate the success of joint ventures. Damanpour et al. (2012) further acknowledged that organisational culture plays a long-lasting role in the effective implementation and management of joint ventures. They also found that the interaction processes of communication, cooperation, and conflict resolution play a key role in the implementation and management of joint ventures and facilitate the management of differences in organisational culture. We next elaborate on the role of shared practices in building ways to mitigate different organisational cultures and enabling the crossing of barriers between the organisations in joint ventures.

8.3 Shared practices

Practice and practices have a multitude of meanings within academic discussion. Gherardi (2009) provides extensive reflections on the different usages and meanings of practice. Practices have been conceptualised somewhat similarly to routines and activities. We consider practices as observable behaviour which is, to some extent, constrained and enabled by a given social context (Van Maanen & Schein, 1977). We adopt the perspective that practice is a system of practices in which knowing is inseparable from doing. By participating in practices, i.e., by doing them, we learn about them, and in the process somehow (re)create and change the practice itself (see Gherardi, 2009; Jyrämä & Äyväri, 2007; Scott, 1987).

The aspects affecting joint ventures, such as organisational structure and culture, are manifested in the shared practice. The ways practices guide the organisation enable or hamper the creation, for example in relation to trust. Inkpen and Currall (2004) highlight how a specific action, i.e., a practice, influences the joint venture, and the ways joint ventures implement practices that relate to trust affects and facilitates learning. Similarly, Damanpour et al. (2010) point out that the practices around building and supporting the interaction processes of communication, cooperation, and conflict resolution are important in joint ventures.

For a joint venture to share practices, there needs to be a process of creating and learning the routines or practices. The ways in which organisations engage to build joint shared practice are multiple. For example, they might build on expert-based apprenticeship practices or create a formal database listing the key competencies needed in order to be able to identify and recognise the different learning mechanisms and required capabilities in practice (Zollo & Winter, 2002).

To conclude, organisational structure and organisational culture affect joint activities and the sharing of knowledge, that is, the ability and willingness to change and create joint identity and brand images (e.g., Ford, 1996; Von Krogh et al., 2000; Zollo & Winter, 2002). In addition, organisational values and practices play a key role in understanding organisations' ability to respond to change (De Long & Fahey, 2000) and new contexts, here in particular the context of cultural joint ventures. Organisational culture that emphasises trust and cooperation (Beamish & Lupton, 2009; Collins & Smith, 2006; Kankanhalli et al., 2005) supports knowledge-sharing and hence the building of a joint understanding of the identity and brand image of a cultural joint venture. Next, we look into these factors in more detail in the context of cultural joint ventures and highlight some of the challenges around them in the case examples.

9 Organisational structure, culture, and practices—enabling or hampering boundary crossing

As discussed above, the organisational structure affects the ways decisions are made, the power relationships, and the ways organisations act, i.e., the practices. The concept of organisational identity is understood here as what is central, distinctive, and enduring about an organisation. It is created through an organisational sensemaking process in which organisational members play a part and the leadership has an important role.

Brand identity is viewed as the external interpretation of the organisation's identity, a message explicitly or implicitly conveyed about the organisation to its stakeholders. The brand identity/image literature has elaborated on the brand identities/images of co-branded products and organisations extensively (Aaker & Joachimsthaler, 2000; see also Basu, 2006; Johansson & Jyrämä, 2016). Here we will investigate the brand in joint ventures through the co-branding perspective. The role of organisational structure and culture in situations of co-branding of organisations with similar products (e.g., concerts), and similar target groups (concert audiences) has received less interest. Johansson and Jyrämä (2016) focus on international music centres that host or have hosted several music ensembles. They argue that a requisite for joint brand identity building is sharing knowledge and joint activities related to the core artistic content (Jyrämä & Johansson, 2017).

Next, we elaborate on the elements of constructing the organisational identities and brands in a cultural joint venture context.

9.1 Centralisation versus decentralisation of partnering organisations

The traditional dichotomy of centralised versus decentralised decision-making is, in fact, a continuum rather than only the two extremes. Centralised/decentralised refers here to the defined power structures, which

DOI: 10.4324/9780429273919-12

are determined often by the size of the organisation, the organisation's cost structures, the effects of technology, and traditions and trends (see Colombo & Delmastro, 2002; see also Madhok et al., 1998 on cost and value). The different functions/departments can be organised as hierarchical or as networks or communities (see Kauppila et al., 2011). The organisational structure as either siloed or networked has been found to affect, for example, knowledge sharing and innovation activity (Kauppila et al., 2011; Bäcklund et al., 2010).

In Part I, we identified that identity-building processes occur at multiple levels and that all the organisational members participate in constructing their views of the organisational identity. In a centralised organisation, it can be assumed that the role of the leadership in managing the organisational identity is more important than in a decentralised one, hence leaving less room for other members of the organisation to actively share their views in the organisational identity formation processes. The effect of the organisational structure on power positions and the role of leadership thus affects the organisational identity in terms of its content and processes.

Similarly, the joining organisations' structures as centralised or decentralised affect how the new entity, the joint venture, will be governed, as well as how the new processes for organisational identity emerge and evolve. As the organisational identity is created through organisational joint discourse and is affected by leadership, the ways in which organisational members share the new organisational identity, or identities, are either enabled or hampered by the organisational structure. The ways in which the hierarchical setting, that is, the power relationships and organisation's departmental structure, provide opportunities for dialogue are by either enabling sensemaking of the new joint identities or leaving them adopting new organisational identities. Another option is that the partnering organisations fight to keep the already adopted views of their organisation as it was before the joint venture.

When looking at the brand image, that is, the perception of the new joint venture from the outside, by the consumers and other stakeholders, the role of the organisational structure has an effect as well. The communication, both explicit and implicit, builds the brand image of the joint venture. This joint brand building conveys to consumers and other stakeholders the key elements of the joint identity. However, if the implicit messages, which are communicated in employee discussions, practices, and news about the joint venture, do not support the desired joint brand image, it most likely will not be adopted by the stakeholders or customers, and instead, a brand image mixing these elements will take place. Therefore, when building the brand image, careful reflection is required on its relationship to the internal joint image.

9.2 Levels of specialisation and expertise—recognised expertise and capabilities

In their comprehensive study, Pugh et al. (1969a) created taxonomies for organisational structures, and an interesting category from the cultural joint ventures point of view is the "professional bureaucracy" that is typically found in organisations with high levels of expertise and professionalism. Cultural organisations, especially in the context of music centres, can easily be categorised as those with high levels of expertise and professionalism. For example, being a musician in a symphony orchestra requires high expertise and specialisation with a musical instrument. The professional bureaucracy described by Pugh et al. (1969a) is characterised by hierarchical structures based on professionalism rather than formal control mechanisms.

In the context of cultural joint ventures, the roles of expertise in creating the joint venture structures and culture can, on the one hand, create easy paths for joint activities. For example, similar backgrounds, education, and shared values (e.g., love of music, to be discussed later in subchapter 9.5), can form paths and bridges for easier communication as well as build trust and relationships across the organisation (cf. discussion on communities of practice by Lave & Wenger, 1991). In addition, musicians playing the same instrument can enable boundary crossing among them, but, on the other hand, can also create competitive situations as each organisation and individual is aiming for the highest level of expertise in their specific fields. What we experienced in the cases included in our study was that, for example, the marketing and communication experts of different partnering organisations were able to collaborate actively already from the beginning of the joint venture, whereas the collaboration between the core artistic activities was more difficult. Thus, the collaboration between marketing experts created a starting point and a further path for other types of collaboration among the partnering organisations.

9.3 The role of parent organisations

The role of an owner organisation—or what we call a parent organisation—is multifaceted in cultural joint ventures. By "parent," we refer to the owner or affiliation of an organisation that is planning to join a cultural joint venture. This also makes a key difference in the situation of mergers and acquisitions in which the merged or acquired organisation becomes part of a new organisation. In the case of joint ventures, the ties to different owners and affiliated organisations remain, and can, in fact, become rather complex.

The parent organisation's values, structure, culture, and practices seem to affect how smoothly a new cultural joint venture is created, but also the ways parent organisations control and manage the joint venture affect its activities (see van der Meer-Kooistra & Kamminga, 2015). The parent company may influence and intervene, for example, through personal choices or control mechanisms, which might be manifested during times of crises, thus creating inefficiencies and other challenges in the formation of a cultural joint venture (Johnson et al., 2001). In addition, as noted earlier, organisational structure and culture are dependent on the parent organisation's structure and culture; similarly, the parent plays a role in the cultural joint venture context (Pugh et al., 1969a; see Marrewijk, 2004 on national culture).

As described, in the context of cultural joint ventures, the relationships between a joint venture and the partnering organisations' parent organisations can become complex. To provide a more concrete view of the potential complexities, we will consider the case of Helsinki Music Centre, in which all the partnering organisations could be considered to have an owner or a parent company: Sibelius Academy, as part of the University of the Arts Helsinki, is a state-funded university; the Helsinki Philharmonic Orchestra (HPO) is a unit of the city of Helsinki; and the Radio Symphony Orchestra (RSO) is owned by the Finnish National Broadcasting Company. Each of these parent or owner organisations affects the joining organisation's ways of management, organisational identity construction, and brand image creation. The HPO players are city employees with rather secure permanent employment, but on the other hand, they might be influenced by the political changes taking place in the city. Likewise, the RSO needs to balance between the support and control of the National Broadcasting Company, for example by offering regular symphony concerts broadcasted on national television and radio, which might impact their choices of concert hours and schedules. These types of ties may also affect the joint activities within the cultural joint venture, in this case the Helsinki Music Centre. In addition, the case of the Baxter Theatre Centre in Cape Town highlights a relationship with the parent organisation. The University of Cape Town is a parent organisation for the Baxter and provides financial support, content through student performances, and a close customer base. Yet, the Baxter Theatre Centre felt that through its historical creation, it was even more significant how the relationship had contributed to the core values of the organisation, its equality and inclusiveness.

Hence, cultural joint ventures need to balance between the joining organisations' cultures but also adapt to their parent organisations' requirements and specificities, which adds an additional dimension to the managerial challenges of the cultural joint ventures. We have conceptualised one of the challenges as a "net of identities" within which the organisational members have multiple sources of identification and identity construction (Johansson & Jyrämä, 2016). In Part I, we described this net of identities through the interorganisational identity construction to emphasise the interrelated nature of identity formation in which the focus is on the different levels of relations and the joint benefits of a cultural joint venture.

9.4 Collaboration-enhanced practices

Jyrämä and Johansson (2017) identified several activities that represent shared practices for cultural joint ventures, namely shared facility services, shared marketing and audience services, and shared artistic activities. They analysed the co-branding processes and concluded that the role of shared artistic activities seems to be vital in building a joint brand identity. Thus, it seems that only by sharing the organisations' core activity—in the case of music centres, the music—the organisations, in fact, shared knowledge linked to their identity construction, which further created a base for joint brand identity building. If only facility or marketing activities were shared between the partnering organisations, it did not seem to create a ground for a joint dialogue on organisational identity building or joint brand identity building.

Therefore, in those organisations that were under the umbrella brand, i.e., the hosting organisations that had their own artistic productions, the brand identity was strongly linked to the hosting organisation's brand identity, whereas where the hosting umbrella organisation was mainly focused on space management and marketing, the sub-brands' organisational identities seemed to play a more important role. In cases where the umbrella organisation engaged in artistic activities, the brand strategy was seen as following the sub-brands or branded house strategies. In contrast, in the cases in which only the facilities or marketing activities were shared, the brand architecture strategy was mainly found within the house of brands or within the fifth identified strategy in which the sub-brands endorsed the organisational brand (Jyrämä & Johansson, 2016).

When considering the previously identified practices, such as the creation of trust, control, and learning, as well as communication, cooperation, and conflict resolution (Damanpour et al., 2012; Inkpen & Currall, 2004), we note that the sharing of everyday practices builds the notion of trust and enables learning through joint experiences. Yet, sharing similar values seems to be key in building shared practices and trust. We next elaborate on the role of values.

9.5 The importance of underlying values—art as the sacred core

We have been looking at organisational identity and brand image, and reflecting on them based on organisational structures, cultures, and practices. In addition, the role of organisational values has been pointed out both in reflections on organisational culture and organisational identity (mentioned previously in this chapter and in Part I). Now, we will take a closer look at the organisational values and their role in cultural joint ventures. First, we will elaborate on the conceptualisation of values, followed by a discussion of the questions: what is art? and what does art as a core value mean for an organisation and a cultural joint venture?

Luonila and Jyrämä (2020) define a value as something that has meaning or use for actors; here, the actors are mainly perceived as the members of an organisation, as well as the stakeholders, such as customers or audiences. In order to better understand what a value means in this context, we need to distinguish value as means of exchange—a simple example being the product and financial value determining the conditions for exchange. The concept "value-in-use" further elaborates on this perspective by arguing that the value only becomes manifested when there is a "use"—i.e., following the simple example, when the product is used. Value-in-context and value-in-networks further emphasise the contextual nature of value created in use. Value-in-use and value-in-context refer to an understanding that value is cocreated by actors and shaped by the context (Äyväri & Jyrämä, 2017; see also Vargo & Lusch, 2014).

Having defined one conceptualisation of value, we now emphasise that in this context, values are not looked at as a means of exchange but as representations of social principles that guide our practices at the individual and organisational levels. We thus adopt a conceptualisation of values as defined in institutional theories, looking at (organisational) practice and the shared beliefs, values, and norms underlying the joint action (see DiMaggio & Powell, 2000; Jyrämä et al., 2021; Scott, 1987). A good example of this is the statement that "art is valuable."

The question "What is art?" has been asked in several disciplines and in the context of several practices. Art has been defined through concepts such as beauty, creativity, newness, innovativeness, aesthetic, and so on (see Hanfling, 1992). These qualities of art connect to experiences of specific kinds, both individual and in a social context. An objective definition of art is hard to find, but it is generally believed that art contains some aspects which enable us to identify similar objects, even art objects from foreign cultures (Jyrämä, 1999).

The recognition of art occurs in a social context, through the art world in aesthetic discussion (see Dickie, 1988), similar to art sociology; in art worlds or fields (see Becker, 1982; Bourdieu, 1984); or within markets (e.g., Jyrämä, 1999; Jyrämä & Äyväri, 2010). To summarise, art can be seen as a product of a specific social context or environment. Art is seen as a product or service of an "art world" which specialises in the production of works of art with symbolic meaning (Becker, 1982).

As discussed earlier, organisational identity is very much attached to organisational values. In the context of joint ventures in the cultural field, the core value can be argued to be the belief that art has intrinsic value and that this is the "sacred core" of the organisation. This core value could be observed, for example, in the discussions that took place during the creation of the Helsinki Music Centre. It was often stated by the arts organisation representatives that they wished to create a house for music, not a shopping centre, not a conference centre, but "a living room for art and music." Similar questions can be observed, for example, in the case of the Harpa Reykjavik Concert Hall and Conference Centre, where the music organisations had the first right to use the spaces, even if Harpa was a popular conference centre and a central visiting point for tourists, featuring shows on the island's natural wonders. Another example is the Baxter Theater Centre in Cape Town, which emphasises two core values, its high-quality art and its commitment to maintaining local connections, building on equality and inclusiveness, with the objective to create linkages with the local South African community. A similar perspective can be seen in the case of the Gran Theatre National, in Lima, Peru, where high-quality art is joined with local culture in the valuing of both traditional classic Western art as well as local art forms.

The cultural joint ventures focused on in this book include only different arts organisations, in which artistic expression is highly valued and art seen as sacred. Thus, the promotion of art can be assumed as a shared value for all, facilitating and enhancing collaboration among the partnering organisations. Yet, these organisations also include service functions, e.g., space rental activities or facility management, which might represent different values and priorities. In addition, there might be differences in how the different genres and forms of art are acknowledged. For example, in the case of the Concertgebouw in the Netherlands, there is a consciously limited focus on unamplified classical music only.

Different perceptions of the arts and artistic quality in the context of cultural joint ventures may also affect the ways organisational members make sense of their own organisation and its brand as well as the venturing organisations and their brands. In many cases, arts and cultural organisations have been created around one key mission, and the expertise of the organisational members has been built around that particular mission. Hence, in the case of cultural joint ventures in which the venture has been formed by joining existing cultural organisations, a challenge is for the organisational members to see and think outside their own core mission.

The following figure summarises the different dimensions that need to be taken into consideration when managing joint ventures in the arts.

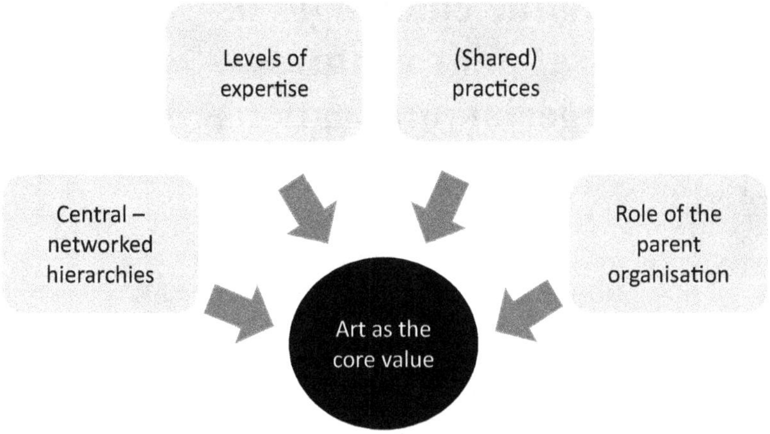

Figure 9.1 The dimensions of managing cultural joint ventures

Next, we reflect on some of the key challenges in brand management that are identified in cultural joint ventures and how to tackle them.

10 Facing the challenges in cultural joint ventures—managerial implications

10.1 Connecting conflicting and similar images—simultaneously building differences and unity

As elaborated on earlier, one of the challenges facing cultural joint ventures is the difficulty in simultaneously building an organisational identity and brand image for the joint venture, and at the same time, maintaining one's own organisational identity and brand image. This challenge is especially crucial in the context in which two similar organisations are joined.

In this case, it is important to define the distinct profiles of the individual organisations and, through the distinctions, maintain the individual brand images—and also decide on the joint areas and the branding for the joint venture. This requires careful joint planning to avoid overlapping content while concurrently building the joint identity and the messages that each organisation wishes to communicate. In practice, within the joint venture, the marketing and content-planning personnel need to meet and share knowledge. This requires a sense of trust and an agreement to meet regularly as an "everyday activity," even if the organisations maintain their own marketing and content departments. Another option is to join the marketing departments into a shared entity and manage both the joint and distinct marketing efforts together. Thus, as pointed out earlier, it is important to create a sense of trust, shared and interdependent control mechanisms, forums for learning through regular communication and cooperation, and mechanisms for open conflict resolution (Damanpour et al., 2012; Inkpen & Currall, 2004).

10.2 Creating joint activities to build content for brand relationships

In addition to sharing marketing and planning activities, building a sense of community and content for the joint brand image requires attention. Sharing

DOI: 10.4324/9780429273919-13

practices in the core activity can be a means for building connections to the brands and actual content for the joint venture's organisational identity and brand image. The shared content, for example concentrated planning for concerts, can be a means to emphasise the joint venture identity and brand. However, this can also lead to centralised decision-making and reduce the relative power position of the joint venture partners. Thus, it is recommended that this be a shared decision, as unequal power relations might result in the joint venture dissolving if any of the partners felt themselves losing their own power position in the process.

On the other hand, shared practices also can be targeted through additional services, such as education activities, specific events, and so on, as doing things together will promote a sense of belonging to the new community, the joint venture. In addition, sharing practices that involve doing activities together, which are also visible to audiences, enable the forming of community, enhance mutual learning, and build ways to create connections between brand images in the eyes of the customers.

10.3 Sorting out identities: cultural centre versus event space?

One of the challenges faced by arts and cultural organisations in joint ventures is the risk of losing their spaces in often architecturally significant buildings and thereby losing their sacred core—the intrinsic value of art. The fear is that they might lose their core existence and mission to conferences, shops, and tourism, for example, which are featured in many cultural joint ventures. These other types of activities and space rentals for different purposes are often a necessity for the operations of the cultural joint ventures to be economically sustainable. The aim is not to bypass the artistic operations but, on the contrary, to enable the diversity of artistic activities that can be offered by the cultural joint ventures (see also Noh and Tolbert, 2019 on complex vs. focused identities).

Some of the cultural joint ventures have consciously decided to control the other activities that are organised within their premises. In addition, many such ventures maintain the power to decide on their own artistic programming prior to allowing space rentals for other activities and actors. In all the cases studied in this book, the cultural joint ventures have endeavoured to maintain their power position to define their individual and joint brand images, in particular when the joint venture brand image has been created through a joint space with high architectural significance. The fear is that other activities not directly related to art may not benefit the brand image visibility or may even reduce the brand image visibility.

11 Capturing the joint and separate organisational identities, brands, and practices

In this chapter, we elaborate on the role of organisational structure and culture in cultural joint ventures, focusing on their organisational identity and brand image. We analyse organisational structure through two dimensions: siloed versus networked. Organisational culture is viewed through organisational practices, with a focus on sharing knowledge and sharing activities.

In Part II, we presented the brand architecture framework and how existing competing brands can be unified or organised under an umbrella or a supporting brand. Here, we will adopt this approach to analyse and categorise the case organisations' branding strategies. Figure 11.1 below summarises the approaches.

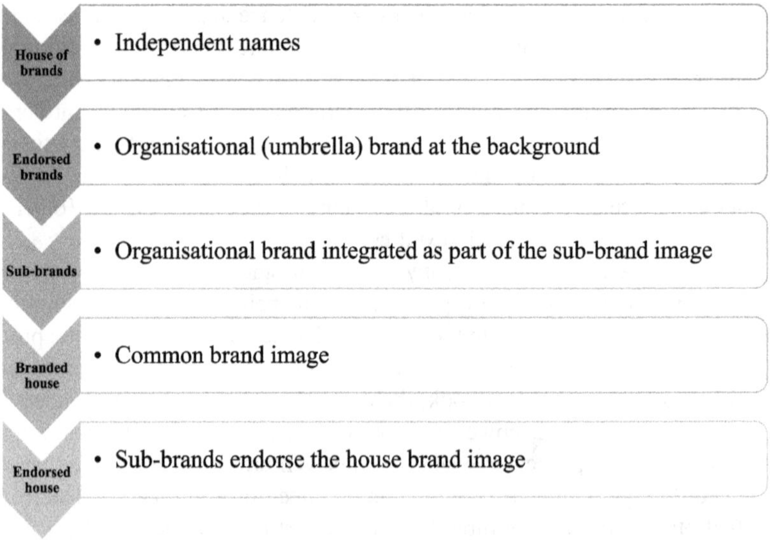
House of brands
• Independent names
Endorsed brands
• Organisational (umbrella) brand at the background
Sub-brands
• Organisational brand integrated as part of the sub-brand image
Branded house
• Common brand image
Endorsed house
• Sub-brands endorse the house brand image

Figure 11.1 A framework for branding strategies

DOI: 10.4324/9780429273919-14

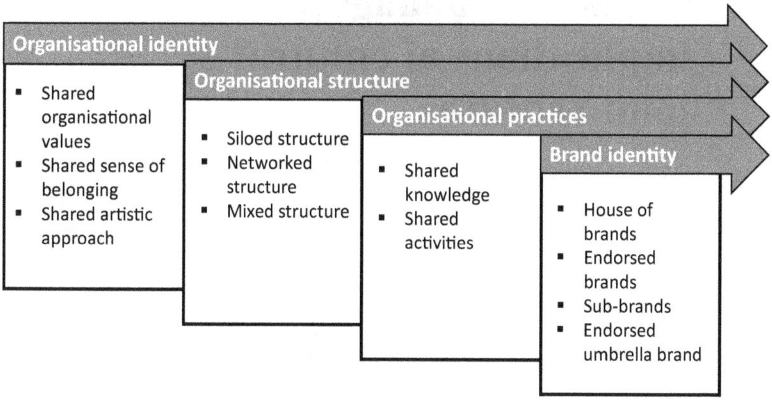

Figure 11.2 Framework for the identity-image view of cultural joint ventures

We propose the following framework for reflecting on the intersection of organisational identities and brand images in the context of cultural joint ventures. This framework has also been used in the following case analyses to identify how the identity-image view has been dealt with and managed in different types and in different phases of cultural joint ventures.

12 Cases and managerial implications of cultural joint ventures

12.1 Case 1: Helsinki Music Centre, Helsinki, Finland

Helsinki Music Centre (HMC) was opened in Helsinki, Finland, in September 2011, and it houses two symphony orchestras, a music university, and a service company, as described in more detail in Parts I and II.

Managerial challenge

The main managerial challenge we were interested in, in terms of managing the identity-image view of the cultural joint venture, was to identify the role of values and structures in managing the first phases of a cultural joint venture.

Organisational structure and culture—identifying organisational identity

Helsinki Music Centre consists of independent organisations that mainly share the facility services. In addition, there is a growing amount of knowledge sharing within the organisations, in terms of, for example, the marketing activities. However, the artistic-activity sharing seems to be lagging behind, even though informal sharing is encouraged, for example by shared lunchrooms. In addition, sometimes musicians visit other ensembles. We suggest that the Helsinki Music Centre can be categorised as an in-between or siloed organisation that is working towards a network organisational structure.

The role of the external view is also vital for identity building in the process of forming a joint venture. Media coverage of the HMC mainly focuses on the architecture of the building and its construction process. The media emphasise particularly the acoustics of the venues, the nature of the building as an architectural entity, and the financial aspect of the investment. In

DOI: 10.4324/9780429273919-15

addition, the media discuss the role and the proportion of different musical genres, which is also reflected in the identity building of the main actors of the HMC. For example, these actors emphasised the need for diversity in the various music genres at the centre and criticised the dominance of classical music. Would it be a venue for music in general or for classical music in particular?

Managing the underlying values, norms, and practices

We identified four key tensions that reflect distinct value dichotomies and can be observed in the differences in the practices and discourses of the partnering organisations (see Table 12.1 below). The first dichotomy concerned the question of using the centre as a "park" for music rather than a "palace" for classical music, as a park would make the centre accessible to a broad range of audiences and appeal to a variety of musical genres. These types of organisational identity perceptions were built on the core value that the HMC exists for the arts and for society. The second tension was around the dichotomy of artistic and economic values, including, for example, the basic operational difference between public and private organisations. Third, the tension between international, national, and local identities reflected the values of building an international reputation or serving local audiences. Finally, the tension between becoming a community or merely users of a joint space reflected different underlying values of wishing to belong or to excel as an organisation.

Table 12.1 Value dichotomies for identity construction in a cultural joint venture

Value dichotomy	*Norms*	*Practices*
Park or palace?	What type of music? What are the opening hours? Any other services?	E.g., due to the need for cost reduction, communal spaces were reduced, but the main concert hall remained unchanged.
Art or economy?	Do we have content other than artistic content? What is the role of profit?	E.g., the scope of renting spaces for external users is under discussion.
International, national, or local?	Who do we serve? What types of activities do we carry out?	E.g., the two orchestras had a different emphasis on educational aims.
Community or space?	Do we work jointly? Do we create joint content?	E.g., the marketing managers have regular meetings and joint activities.

The joint practices, such as having regular meetings, seemed to affect the values and views on cooperation, as well as building a joint community identity in HMC. The existing organisations' strategic decisions and practices also affected the identity construction, as in the case of being either internationally or locally oriented.

We identified different values and meanings attached to the cultural joint venture and how these created tensions between the partnering organisations. First, the main actors in the new HMC seemed to want to maintain their own distinct identities, which was perceived as essential for survival: *why have two symphony orchestras if they are the same?* The music university also seemed to emphasise its own distinct identity as a university by stressing that *it is not only a concert hall.*

It seemed that the partnering organisations struggled with what we call a "network of identities." They identified with their background organisations, their immediate organisation, and the new joint venture. Interestingly, however, these identities, even though sometimes conflicting, seemed to be intertwined and exist simultaneously.

The partnering organisations' visions and fears for the new cultural joint venture reflected the four value dichotomies mentioned previously. The value dichotomies were built on shared or non-shared values that guided organisational practices and identity views. We also identified a fear of changing identity rather than a fear of losing it. For example, the fear of changing identity was related to the question of whether the HMC should be an active venue full of people and music or an empty palace for classical music, as well as that the HMC would be taken over by entirely nonmusical activities, such as conferences, and thus be governed primarily by for-profit missions and goals. However, the underlying value, the love for music, might enable joint identity building for the music centre as a community unified by music. Nevertheless, it remains to be seen how the service organisation will take part in this and whether it will share the values as the main actors. Hence, we emphasise that the shared values are important in shared identity building, and that the shared value base facilitates cooperation. It seems that only by agreeing on a shared value base can joint identity building as a community begin.

We want to emphasise that the identified value dichotomies are not exclusive. The same person or organisational actor can have conflicting values, such as art versus economy, without having any inner conflicts. Nevertheless, identifying these value dichotomies can provide managers with insights to help them cope with the identity processes in joint ventures.

However, it seems that even if the core value is shared, there are still challenges in building a joint venture with a joint identity. The tensions include topics such as the genres of music, the choice between a "shopping mall" type of venue and a "park filled with people and music," and the role of activities other than music. The identified values seem to be at the core for individuals, whereas some of the value statements guiding the everyday actions may be at different levels and thus easier to change, while still guiding the actors' views and practices. We propose that when analysing organisational identity construction, there is a need to consider the different layers of value statements and their role in the shared practices.

Managing the perceived brand identity and co-branding strategies

As analysed in a previous study (Jyrämä et al., 2015), Helsinki Music Centre had strong independent organisational brand identities that seemed to endorse the umbrella brand of the music centre. However, it would be interesting to see whether this will change as the joint venture gains more experience and opportunities to find identities of its own. Even if the joint activities with marketing supported the collaboration of different in-house actors, it did not contribute to the creation of a joint brand. Helsinki Music Centre had decided not to stage artistic productions of its own, which seemed to play a central role in the process of creating a joint brand.

12.2. Case 2: Copenhagen Concert Hall, Copenhagen, Denmark

Copenhagen Concert Hall was opened in 2009 and is the architectural masterpiece of French architect Jean Nouvel. The concert complex consists of four halls, with the main hall seating 1,800 people. Events at the Copenhagen Concert Hall range in terms of size and genre: small-scale jazz concerts in the foyer; chamber music, choral, and rock and pop concerts in the three smaller concert halls; and symphony concerts, guest appearances, and large-scale rhythmic concerts in the large concert hall (for a more detailed description and analysis of the case, please see Jyrämä & Johansson, 2017).

At the time of the study, the Copenhagen Concert Hall housed eight different orchestras and vocal ensembles: Danish National Symphony Orchestra, Danish National Chamber Orchestra, Danish National Vocal Ensemble, Danish National Concert Choir, Danish National Girls' Choir, Danish National Children's Choir, Danish National Sprouts Choir, and DR Big Band.

The Copenhagen Concert Hall seems to have a strong connection to its mother organisation, the Danish Broadcasting Corporation. It also has joint marketing, educational programmes, and customer services for the orchestras and choir.

Managerial challenge

The main managerial challenge was how to build an endorsed brand architecture strategy simultaneously for two entities: the concert hall and the radio.

Managerial response

The challenge of connecting two brand images to an organisational brand is not uncommon in cultural fields. Several orchestras and ensembles have the same situation internationally, as, on the one hand, they connect to their "parent" organisation, often a national broadcasting company or a city, and, on the other hand, to the venue, the concert hall, which is their home in the physical context.

The parent organisation has strong historical roots with the organisation and its brand image and is usually their main funder. The venue, the concert hall, is connected strongly in loyal customers' minds to the overall experience of a concert or event of the organisation, and hence is both emotionally and functionally connected to the brand image.

The Copenhagen Concert Hall has solved the challenge, by creating a joint visual image for the music entities and using the "mother organisation" in brand names in similar visual ways, thus providing ways to connect to both potential brand endorsers.

Organisational structure and culture—identifying organisational identity

The Copenhagen Concert Hall has a strong connection to its parent organisation, the Danish Broadcasting Corporation. However, it used to consist of independent suborganisations, each of which had its own strong identity. In early 2000, this changed with a change in leadership. After that, each entity was reorganised into a joint organisation. This resulted in certain restructurings of collaborative practices aimed at building shared objectives for the concert hall. Even if some overlaps with the music ensembles were recognised, it was not perceived as a significant issue. Instead, the need for a strong back office under one administration became the basis for building a joint identity. The Copenhagen Concert Hall might not fit in either the preconceived organisational forms or in the siloed and networked ones, as it seems to be emerging into one joint organisation, even more shared than in a networked one.

Perceived brand identity and co-branding strategies

At the time of the study, the Copenhagen Concert Hall seemed to have adopted an endorsed brand architecture strategy. It faced challenges in its branding due to the economic difficulties in the past but managed to create a strong brand for the concert hall itself. It aimed to have an endorsed brand architecture strategy that connected the concert hall's brand to the existing brands of the partnering organisations. Thus, it ended up having distinct organisational sub-brands that are strongly connected to the concert hall brand. Many of the sub-brands seem to connect to the Danish Broadcasting Corporation as well.

The Copenhagen Concert Hall has adopted an umbrella strategy in its branding. It has faced challenges in this due to economic difficulties in the past but has now created a strong umbrella brand for the concert hall itself. However, it aims to have an endorsed strategy that connects the concert hall's brand to the existing brands of the music ensembles. Thus, we categorise it in the sub-brand category, with clear sub-brands, but which are strongly connected to the umbrella brand. In addition to their connection to the concert hall brand, many of the sub-brands connect to the Danish radio as well. Moreover, the concert hall has considered building different spaces for each ensemble within the hall, with their own names and images.

12.3 Case 3: Harpa, Reykjavík, Iceland

Harpa Reykjavík Concert Hall and Conference Centre was opened in 2011. Diversity was described as the value at the forefront in all activities, so that all musical genres could find a home in Harpa. Various music festivals are held regularly in the building, including Iceland Airwaves, Reykjavík Midsummer Music, Dark Music Days, Reykjavík Arts Festival, Reykjavík Jazz Festival, Sónar Reykjavík, Tectonics, and Harpa International Music Academy. At the time of the study, Harpa was the home for three in-house ensembles: the Iceland Symphony Orchestra, the Icelandic Opera, and the Reykjavík Big Band. In addition to its concerts, Harpa rented spaces for many other concerts, events, and conferences (for a more detailed analysis of the case, see Jyrämä & Johansson, 2017).

Managerial challenge

The managerial challenge we were interested in was how to balance a brand image with the differing aims and target groups. In other words, was Harpa a home for cultural organisations or a tourist destination?

Managerial response

Harpa's role was to be a venue for music and culture as well as conferences, meetings, and gatherings, both Icelandic and foreign. Its objective was furthermore to be a cultural centre for all Icelanders in the centre of Reykjavík and a destination for foreign and domestic travellers who were interested in learning more about the building, the services offered, and the building's architecture and art. The Harpa Concert and Conference Centre was expected to support itself through its operations such that no further public funding would be required other than that provided for in the owners' agreements and policies.

An in-house management company, Hörpustrengir ehf., was established in December 2013 with the purpose of producing selected events to mark the footprints of the Icelandic music and cultural scene, which would not be possible without this involvement. Events were usually produced in conjunction with selected partners, and the company aimed to avoid holding events that would be in direct competition with the event holders and permanent users of the building.

Organisational structure and culture—identifying organisational identity

Harpa Concert Hall and Conference Centre is run as a public organisation and is owned jointly by the state (54%) and the City of Reykjavík (46%). The operations of Harpa are governed by the Board of Directors, and the operational management of the hall is the responsibility of the managing director of Harpa. The operations of Harpa are divided between concerts and conference marketing, as well as the stage and technique functions. There is also Harpa's Arts Board, consisting of representatives from each resident ensemble and different artist associations. The Arts Board is an important element within Harpa, as this group of people provide long-term artistic leadership and collaboration for the venue. In the beginning, the different resident ensembles tended to work independently without much collaboration, but this has changed over the years, in particular with the launch of the Arts Board.

Perceived brand identity and co-branding strategies

Harpa seemed to have applied an umbrella brand from the beginning of its operations. Harpa itself was chosen as the overarching brand identity, which was emphasised in the international documents, organisational talks, and marketing material. Also, the visual identity of Harpa was united from the beginning, although this was not an easy decision and process for the resident ensembles. For example, the colour yellow is used throughout the internal and external marketing material and has become a key element of brand identity. Even if the resident orchestras and opera have their sub-brands, they are very strongly connected to Harpa as an umbrella brand.

Harpa's brand image was created through several elements: its signature architecture, its cultural and artistic content, and its relationship to the national image of the Island.

12.4 Case 4: The Baxter Theatre Centre, Cape Town, South Africa

The Baxter Theatre Centre is a multicultural arts centre that presents its own productions and hosts several visiting art productions. Its activities encompass all types of professional entertainment—music, drama, ballet, opera, and intimate theatre. It was opened in 1977 with a strong mission of equality and inclusion. The objective was to reflect the cultures of all the people of South Africa and develop an interactive relationship with the local and university communities.

The Baxter is the home for University of Cape Town (UCT) performing-art students' productions in e.g., classical music and opera, and it maintains a close relationship with the university as a parent organisation. UCT is seen as contributing to the content and as providing an audience. The Baxter is located near the university campus in the Southern Suburbs of Cape Town. It has a world-class theatre and concert hall, as well as a studio stage, rehearsal rooms, offices, a restaurant and bars, and an impressive, spacious foyer.

The Baxter was a pillar of hope during the apartheid era as through its strong relationship with UCT, the theatre was able to present multiracial, progressive work at a time when all other nonracial interactivity was banned or censored. This guiding value base is still strongly present in the organisation.

Organisational structure and culture—identifying organisational identity

The Baxter Theatre Centre is part of the University of Cape Town, which partly funds its activities. In addition, its income comes from ticket sales and renting the premises for other art productions. The Baxter staff benefits from the organisational support of the UCT, for example its HR services, but it has its own artistic, technical, and marketing staff. Baxter was expected to support itself through its operations so that no public funding would be required other than that provided by the university. However, this led to extensive opening hours in which it was engaged in its own productions as well as overseeing multiple rental organisations. Rental organisations were selected case by case among art organisations and productions. The Baxter met these demands but also actively pursues art productions, mainly in the local scene, that fits its profile. The Baxter also provided professional support and advice to rental productions in order to maintain the professional quality, the fit with their mission, and the marketing support to ensure a sufficient amount of ticket sales and audience. The Baxter Theatre Centre kept the core artistic programming in its own hands. Moreover, it created an international reputation through visits to key festivals and international tours.

The main focus of the Baxter Theatre Centre is theatre, but it also hosts musical events, and its collaboration with UCT is strongly focused on classical music and opera. In all its productions, it aims to connect to its mission and to build inclusiveness through its content, affordable prices, and welcoming atmosphere. Thus, its organisational identity, and especially its value base, is emphasised in many ways.

Perceived brand identity and co-branding strategies

The Baxter Theatre Centre seems to apply an umbrella brand strategy. The Baxter as a home for its own productions and those of rental organisations is an overarching brand identity, which can be seen in its selection of content and is also integrated in its marketing material. Even if the rental producers have their own brands, they are connected to the Baxter as an umbrella brand. As part of its organisational identity, its history and value base is made explicit in its external communications as well.

References

Aaker, D. A., & Joachimsthaler, E. (2000). The brand relationship spectrum: The key to the brand architecture challenge. *California Management Review*, *42*(4), 8–23.

Äyväri, A., & Jyrämä, A. (2017). Rethinking value proposition tools for living labs. *Journal of Service Theory and Practice, 27*(5), 1024–1039.

Bäcklund, P., Jyrämä, A., & Väisänen, H. (2010). "Nyt innovoidaan!" Helsingin kaupungin henkilöstön kokemuksia kehittämistyöstä.

Basu, K. (2006). Merging brands after mergers. *California Management Review*, *48*(4), 28–40.

Beamish, P. W., & Lupton, N. C. (2009). Managing joint ventures. *Academy of Management Perspectives*, *23*, 75–94.

Becker, H. S. (1982). *Art worlds*. Berkeley, Los Angeles, CA and London: University of California Press.

Bourdieu, P. (1984). *Distinction—A social critic of the judgement of taste*. Cambridge, MA: Harvard University Press.

Child, J. (1972). Organizational structure, environment, performance: The role of strategic choice. *Sociology, 6*, 1–22.

Collins, C. J., & Smith, K. G. (2006). Knowledge exchange and combination: The role of human resource practices in the performance of high-technology firms. *Academy of Management Journal*, *49*(3), 544–560.

Colombo, M. G., & Delmastro, M. (2002). The determinants of organizational change and structural inertia: Technological and organizational factors. *Journal of Economics & Management Strategy*, *11*(4), 595–635.

Damanpour, F., Devece, C., Chen, C. C., & Pothukuchi, V. (2012). Organizational culture and partner interaction in the management of international joint ventures in India. *Asia Pacific Journal of Management*, *29*(2), 453–478.

De Chernatony, L. (1999). Brand management through narrowing the gap between brand identity and brand reputation. *Journal of Marketing Management*, *15*(1–3), 157–179.

De Long, D. W., & Fahey, L. (2000). Diagnosing cultural barriers to knowledge management. *Academy of Management Perspectives*, *14*(4), 113–127.

Dickie, G. (1988). *Evaluating art*. Philadelphia, PA, USA: Temple University Press.

DiMaggio, P. J., & Powell, W. W. (2000). The iron cage revisited institutional isomorphism and collective rationality in organizational fields. In *Economics meets sociology in strategic management*. New Haven, CT, USA: Emerald Group Publishing Limited.

Fey, C. F., & Beamish, P. W. (2001). Organizational climate similarity and performance: International joint ventures in Russia. *Organization Studies*, *22*(5), 853–882.

Ford, C. M. (1996). A theory of individual creative action in multiple social domains. *Academy of Management review, 21*(4), 1112–1142.

Gherardi, S. (2009). Introduction: The critical power of the practice lens. *Management Learning*, *40*(2), 115–128.

Gorondutse, A. H., & Hilman, H. (2018). Does organizational culture matter in the relationship between trust and SMEs performance. *Management Decision*, 57(7), 1638–1658.

Hanfling, O. (1992). *Philosophical aesthetics—An introduction*. Oxford: Blackwell Publishers.

Hatch, M. J. (1993). The dynamics of organizational culture. *Academy of Management Review*, *18*(4), 657–693.

Hatch, M. J., & Schultz, M. (1997). Relations between organizational culture, identity and image. *European Journal of Marketing, 31*(5), 356–365.

Hatch, M. J., & Schultz, M. (2002). The dynamics of organisational identity. *Human Relations*, *55*(8), 989–1018.

Hatch, M. J., & Zilber, T. (2012). Conversation at the border between organizational culture theory and institutional theory. *Journal of Management Inquiry*, *21*(1), 94–97.

Hofstede, G., Neuijen, B., Ohayv, D. D., & Sanders, G. (1990). Measuring organizational cultures: A qualitative and quantitative study across twenty cases. *Administrative Science Quarterly*, 286–316.

Hsu, C. K., Marsh, R. M., & Mannari, H. (1983). An examination of the determinants of organizational structure. *American Journal of Sociology*, *88*(5), 975–996.

Inkpen, A. C., & Currall, S. C. (2004). The coevolution of trust, control, and learning in joint ventures. *Organization Science*, *15*(5), 586–599.

Johansson, T., & Jyrämä, A. (2016). Network of organizational identities in the formation of a cultural joint venture: A case study of the Helsinki Music Centre. *International Journal of Arts Management*, 67–78.

Johnson, J. L., Cullen, J. B., Sakano, T., & Bronson, J. W. (2001). Drivers and outcomes of parent company intervention in IJV management: A cross-cultural comparison. *Journal of Business Research*, *52*(1), 35–49.

Jyrämä, A. (1999). *Contemporary art markets: Structure and practices. A study on art galleries in Finland, Sweden, France, and Great Britain*. Helsinki School of Economics. Helsinki, Finland.

Jyrämä. A. and Johansson, T. (2017). *Co-branding an identity – international comparison of Music Centres*. 14th International Conference on Arts and Cultural management, June 24-June 28, 2017; Peking University, Peking, China.

Jyrämä, A., & Äyväri, A. (2007). Fostering learning—the role of mediators. *Knowledge Management Research & Practice*, *5*(2), 117–125.

Jyrämä, A., & Äyväri, A. (2010). Marketing contemporary visual art. *Marketing Intelligence & Planning, 28*(6), 723–735.

Jyrämä, A., Kajalo, S., Johansson, T., & Siren, A. (2015). Arts organizations and branding: Creating a new joint brand for three arts organizations. *The Journal of Arts Management, Law, and Society*, *45*(3), 193–206.

Jyrämä, A., Kiitsak-Prikk, K., & Äyvari, A. (2021). The art organisation's societal engagement—do the artist's values matter? *European Journal of Cultural Management and Policy, 11*(1), 20–30.

Kankanhalli, A., Tan, B. C., & Wei, K. K. (2005). Contributing knowledge to electronic knowledge repositories: An empirical investigation. *MIS Quarterly*, 113–143.

Kauppila, O. P., Rajala, R., & Jyrämä, A. (2011). Knowledge sharing through virtual teams across borders and boundaries. *Management Learning*, *42*(4), 395–418.

Lave, J., & Wenger, E. (1991). *Situated learning. Legitimate peripheral participation*. Cambridge, UK: Cambridge University Press.

Luonila, M., & Jyrämä, A. (2020). Does co-production build on co-creation or does co-creation result in co-producing? *Arts and the Market, 10*(1), 1–17.

Madhok, A., & Tallman, S. B. (1998). Resources, transactions and rents: Managing value through interfirm collaborative relationships. *Organisation Science*, *9*(3), 326–339.

Marrewijk, V. A. (2004). The management of strategic alliances: Cultural resistance. Comparing the cases of a Dutch telecom operator in the Netherlands, Antilles and Indonesia. *Culture and Organisation*, *10*(4), 303–314.

Noh, S., & Tolbert, P. S. (2019). Organizational identities of U.S. art museums and audience reactions. *Poetics*, *72*, 94–107.

Pothukuchi, V., Damanpour, F., Choi, J., Chen, C. C., & Park, S. H. (2002). National and organizational culture differences and international joint venture performance. *Journal of International Business Studies*, *33*(2), 243–265.

Pugh, D. S., Hickson, D. J., & Hinings, C. R. (1969a). An empirical taxonomy of structures of work organizations. *Administrative Science Quarterly*, 115–126.

Pugh, D. S., Hickson, D. J., Hinings, C. R., & Turner, C. (1969b). The context of organization structures. *Administrative Science Quarterly*, 91–114.

Scott, W. R. (1987). The adolescence of institutional theory. *Administrative Science Quarterly*, 493–511.

Shu, C., Jin, J. L., & Zhou, K. Z. (2017). A contingent view of partner coopetition in international joint ventures. *Journal of International Marketing*, *25*(3), 42–60.

van der Meer-Kooistra, J., & Kamminga, P. E. (2015). Joint venture dynamics: The effects of decisions made within a parent company and the role of joint venture management control. *Management Accounting Research*, *26*, 23–39.

Van Maanen, J. E., & Schein, E. H. (1977). *Toward a theory of organizational socialization*. Cambridge, MA: The MIT Press.

Vargo, S. L., & Lusch, R. F. (2014). Inversions of service-dominant logic. *Marketing Theory*, *14*(3), 239–248.

Von Krogh, G., Ichijo, K., & Nonaka, I. (2000). *Enabling knowledge creation: How to unlock the mystery of tacit knowledge and release the power of innovation*. Oxford: Oxford University Press on Demand.

Weber, M. (1994). *Weber: Political writings*. Cambridge: Cambridge University Press.

Zollo, M., & Winter, S. G. (2002). Deliberate learning and the evolution of dynamic capabilities. *Organization Science*, *13*(3), 339–351.

Part IV

The future of cultural joint ventures

Part IV of the book considers the future of cultural joint ventures and the implications for a new era of collaboration. Cultural organisations face so-called megatrends, which create both challenges and new opportunities in the entire cultural and creative sector, as well as in many other businesses and institutions. The major tendencies towards internationalisation, digitalisation, changes in customer behaviour, and new types of organisations with changing business models all have been strongly affected by the COVID-19 pandemic. This and other worldwide crises have impacted many of the existing tendencies in the field and accelerated some, such as digitalisation.

Along with the challenges and negative effects of the pandemic, some new opportunities have unfolded, and therefore we can foresee new trends emerging. For that reason, we examine the "post-COVID" era of cultural joint ventures and the changes that affect interorganisational collaboration in the long run. The tendencies towards various hybrid forms in national and international collaboration and the changes in the way organisations and customers behave are also considered. We explore the future prospects, as well as the requirements and potential challenges, of leading and managing such hybrid forms of collaboration in the context of cultural joint ventures.

DOI: 10.4324/9780429273919-16

13 Key future trends for cultural joint ventures

13.1 Changes in organisational forms

The cultural and creative sector is known for its large proportion of micro-sized organisations and freelancers. OECD's report (2020) stated that the sector is largely composed of micro-firms, nonprofit organisations, and creative professionals, often operating on the margins of financial sustainability. Large public and private cultural institutions and organisations depend on this dynamic cultural ecosystem for the provision of creative goods and services. Yet, we have witnessed how global crises, including the pandemic, have had the worst effect on freelancers and the self-employed within the cultural and creative workforce. It has been said that global crises reveal the fragility of the cultural sector due to its domination by micro-businesses, informal work practices, and limited tangible assets (Buchoud et al., 2021). For the cultural joint ventures, this often means that the number of collaborators decreases as the individual organisations try to survive and keep their own staff employed. On the other hand, when the pandemic forced cultural organisations and freelancers to halt their activities, many adapted to new digital distribution formats and channels. Hence, the cultural sector witnessed an increased sectoral unity through numerous joint actions and movements (IDEA Consult et al., 2021). Therefore, we argue that the future of collaborations will be more and more dependent on the policies supporting the freelance, project-based, and self-reliant part of the ecosystem.

At the same time, we have witnessed in recent decades how the boundaries between the public, private, and third sector are becoming blurred, leading to hybrid organisational forms (Ruusuvirta, 2019). In the last couple of decades, digitalisation, internationalisation, and professionalisation have been understood to have a strong influence on traditional organisational forms (Hagoort, 2003). Another layer of complexity has been added to the collaborative organisational context, in which so-called quangos or quasi-NGOs are involved. We have already experienced and will probably see

DOI: 10.4324/9780429273919-17

more cases of these quasi-autonomous cultural organisations collaborating with other types of organisations. The identity-image building processes are affected by cultural ventures in which the parent company is not a purely public arts organisation but a hybrid organisation. Thus, heterogeneity inside these organisations might contribute to forming new types of joint identities. Even more, these hybrid organisational forms may offer a more flexible and sustainable way of responding to change. Therefore, these types of organisations might be considered as viable collaboration partners.

Dynamic organisational forms have always been a reflection of larger societal changes. New organisational structures develop along with the emergence of new practices and business models required for adapting to the ever-changing reality. The cultural and creative sector is prone to network-based organisational structures, and the post-pandemic "new reality" could foster this. According to Hagoort (2003), in the network-based organisational structure, the project teams are strongly connected to specific customer groups, co-producers, and partners. Alongside the strengthening pool of freelancers and collaboration forms of different types of partners across borders, network-based organisations can often be a logical path of development. Cultural organisations with facilities or spaces often become a platform—the facilitators of collaborative projects, engaging an irregular and freelance workforce. Lacking large, formal organisational structures, these types of organisations are often smaller, more flexible, and considered to be more resilient in times of crises, even if their individual members might be hit harder (Betzler et al., 2021).

When these network-based organisations form strategic alliances, the management and branding of the joint ventures become more complex and multidimensional. Joint branding could be, on the one hand, an integration of clear sub-brands (house of brands approach), as the identities formed inside the network-based organisations might not be looking in the same direction, or else more unified in cases where the joining actors do not have their own strong brands aimed at the end customers. In addition, there could be more benefits to developing joint initiatives with network-based and hybrid organisations: that is, cross-fertilisation between different types of organisations in the cultural sector supports the development of creative clusters (Plaza & Haarich, 2017). Joining under creative clusters, in which a common identity and brand is "a critical glue" holding the cluster together (Creative Clusters, 2022), is just one of many potential developments of cultural joint ventures. This leads us to believe that the new reality of arts and cultural organisations and their changing organisational forms pave multiple ways for the branding of joint ventures.

Indeed, in challenging conditions, the alternative approach of choosing collaboration partners outside the cultural field or among the traditional set of potential collaborators is probably a tendency to keep an eye on. For example, IDEA Consult et al.'s (2021) report stated that during the COVID-19 crisis, many cultural and creative workers and organisations demonstrated their innovative power to experiment with possible alternatives, often in collaboration with new partners. Indeed, the cultural and creative sector indicated a new direction in which collaboration increased with new types of partners, particularly with partners having technical expertise in the online mediation of cultural offerings, especially in a global context.

From the cultural joint ventures point of view, this was a promising turn that enabled the formation of multiple partnerships from different parts of the world. Thus, digital collaboration has become a norm, accelerated by the pandemic and the fact that remote work has proven to be successful in many types of organisations. Naturally, there are certain activities that cannot be replaced by online platforms but, on the other hand, we should not just try to get back to the ways things were done in the pre-pandemic times.

To summarise, in choosing different types of organisations and different sector organisations as collaborative partners, we might see in the future more informal joint ventures that involve partnering organisations from different parts of the world. Building on the potential of digital collaborations, these borderless joint ventures have great potential. Organisations from different countries may, for instance, join their activities for a certain period of time, for a certain theme to develop, or for certain artistic content and audience engagement activities to be developed together.

From the managerial point of view, this requires skills in leading intercultural virtual teams, an understanding of more varied audiences, and knowledge of international arts funding (both public and private sources). The identity-image view of cultural joint ventures will most probably increase in complexity, and thus new studies will be needed in the future.

13.2 Changes in practices

The reality for organisations in the arts and cultural field is increasingly complex. Aside from the changing organisational structures, the way of functioning has been affected by rapid change as well. We have witnessed how times of crises have led to new opportunities: for example, innovative solutions for cultural services emerged rather quickly at the beginning of the COVID-19 pandemic. Intensified consumption and production of digital cultural content, which was largely due to the impossibility of occupying physical cultural spaces during the pandemic, is one of the adaptations that has taken place in the cultural sector, both among its audiences and its producers (UNESCO, 2021). Also, the existing cultural joint ventures were able to find another level of collaboration as they were forced to unite their knowledge and practices in order to cope with the continuously changing requirements and instructions from the authorities. For instance, the partnering organisations of the Helsinki Music Centre coordinated their instructions to audiences in order to provide a coherent image to their customers. This is just one example of many. Complying with the new type of uncertainty of constantly changing restrictions provided an opportunity to build stronger ties between the partners in joint ventures and led the way to new collaborations.

In responding to the demands of the new reality, cultural organisations have redefined their success. The number of sold tickets or physical seats filled is no longer the only performance indicator. Revenue from online streaming and digital visits has become equally important to many organisations. At the same time, the number of hours spent at the workplace is no longer a determinant of achieved goals. The indicator of successful practice has become rather the number of adaptations and the speed of responsiveness to the changing needs and contexts. Moreover, as the environment of cultural organisations is ever-changing with artificial intelligence, the platform economy, ageing populations, economic crises, environmental challenges, and the rise of populism across the EU (KEA & PPMI, 2019, p. 23), cultural organisations' success is determined by their ability to confront and respond to these challenges with rapid adaptation in practices and business models.

We have witnessed how the cultural and creative sector quickly adapted to the COVID-19 crisis and faced the market restrictions with joint forces and temporary support measures in many countries (Compendium, 2021). Subsequently, the sector has had to cope with the negative aspects of the temporality of these support measures and adapt to being cut off from the safety network provided by public funding. After the support measures expired for the cultural sector, another quick adaptation was required to cope with the new reality and find quick ways to survive. Arts and cultural organisations, including joint ventures, have been forced to find their way out of their dependency on these short-term support boosts. Managing the collaborations beyond the crisis support systems might lead to critical situations for some organisations, but to new emerging solutions for others.

The lasting effect of these changes and crises is the emergence of new business models in order to remain sustainable. In turbulent times, a revision of the value proposition and a diversification of revenue streams, along with reaching new customer segments, can be critical in terms of the viability of cultural organisations. For example, in order to increase the revenue streams in the context of crisis and limitation due to the pandemic, the Helsinki Music Centre started to rent its main hall for private gatherings with a limited number of people. It is assumed that the general trend is the exponential transformation of business models, with the focus on solving problems for the masses and building information-based services, relying more on user-generated content and a community of fans (van der Pijl, 2018).

To deliver value, organisations seek multiple revenue streams and additional private sources of finance, which has led to expectations towards policy makers to provide incentives to stimulate private investments (KEA & PPMI, 2019). In addition, the new developments in business models include a leaner approach, with rapid cycles of experimentation and learning (van der Pijl, 2018). An example of change in the key activities is the change in concert formats: due to the pandemic restrictions, some concerts were shortened to approximately one hour without an intermission. On the one hand, this is an example of "optimisation" and adaptation to the circumstances, while, on the other hand, it might change the tradition of two-part longer concerts with an intermission.

Even though in arts and culture the scalability and automatisation of core processes is not always possible, for example in relation to the so-called Baumol's cost disease (Baumol & Bowen, 1966), the adoption of design thinking in these organisations is becoming more common in order to find new ways of serving audiences. Often, these new practices concern side activities, while the core activities (such as the performance itself) remain unchanged. However, depending on the art field, the core activities could also be reviewed and the organisational practices for art productions renewed. Digitalisation and new technologies are becoming more available and common in core artistic production. For example, the use of augmented reality and virtual reality (AR and VR) can inspire artists in their creative process, and we see more extraordinary artworks using these technologies. Interesting future trends, such as voice control, gesture control, the Internet of Things or the Internet of Everything, blockchain-driven services, and the emergence of quantum computing (Dufva, 2020a) are all fertile ground for new core activities in the arts and culture sector.

In the performing arts, live streaming offers many new perspectives on creation, with works which are specially curated for the online environment. In museums, technology such as 3D laser scanning will contribute to better protecting cultural heritage (KEA & PPMI, 2019). Artwork created with or about these technological advancements, or artwork curated specially for online environments, offers an endless source of innovation and collaboration in the future. For example, immersive theatre is a new form of collaboration between theatres, museums, and the gaming industry (European Commission, 2021).

Along with the need to "connect physical and multiple digital outlets to enhance the value of their core offering" (van der Pijl, 2018), arts and cultural organisations continuously seek new collaborations for hybrid platforms and channels of distribution. Marketing and distribution are definitely the parts of business models which have been affected by digitalisation the most. Digitalisation is constantly transforming the working processes and operations, especially related to audience development, ticketing, and communication; physical distribution has been gradually replaced by digital distribution with the emergence of data-driven marketing (KEA & PPMI, 2019).

We see this trend as deepening and becoming an integrated, essential part of cultural organisations, especially since the audience expectations and the norms, rules, and practices of the newest generations have changed drastically. COVID-19 accelerated the change in sociological patterns (KEA, 2020) that are familiar to the younger generation, who are more individualistic and focused on their private life, with smaller-scale communities relying on digital and virtual networks. Their ability to concentrate is also different and has been shaped by the use of images and pedagogies that enable quick learning and experience. The pandemic has affected collective behaviours and cultures to the same extent as Scripture or printing in their original times. In order for cultural institutions to remain relevant and contribute to social empowerment (KEA, 2020), the established cultural institutions or business structures need to build adaptive structures and practices, taking into account the reality of the customer segments.

We have experienced changes in audience performance, such as irrational consumer behaviour—from panic-buying and hoarding to postponed purchases—face coverings, and social distancing (see Khlystova et al., 2022), which all affect the practices of cultural ventures and will continue to do so during the critical times in the future. The live-streaming, limitless access to creative content, high-quality recordings, etc., are changing the customers' experience, demand, and consumption (Khlystova et al., 2022). Audiences have quickly learned new ways of consuming arts and cultural offerings and have proven that the adaptation to crisis solutions and the re-adaptation to regular ones can be handled by new audiences and loyal ones as well. Also, consumers take the democratising of their sources of information for granted.

Different customer segments expect the cultural organisations to utilise the most relevant platforms and technology to provide comprehensive accessibility, engagement, and convenience. This has been an increasing tendency; for example, museums and galleries have increasingly created AR/VR apps to attract more visitors (European Commission, 2021). The trend of using AR/VR to engage with the audience leads us to believe that there will be new ventures emerging in this way. In addition, recent technology solutions promote equality by helping blind people see, or giving physically weak people more strength (Dufva, 2020a), and, therefore, cultural organisations are expected to update their audience services constantly. The extensive digital literacy in society builds expectations towards cultural organisations to correspond to the needs of audiences. On the other hand, customers, especially youth, are more vulnerable due to their dependency on digital solutions, complex systems, and the isolation caused by digital communication (Dufva, 2020a). Hence, it is the ethical and social responsibility of cultural organisations to avoid the misuse of technology and instead create joint ventures to find constructive and responsive solutions.

Also, the values of the new generations related to the so-called "green shift" has created new opportunities and challenges for cultural joint ventures. The environmental footprint of cultural organisations deserves more attention now than ever. Striving for good practices and the execution of innovative initiatives in this regard may lead the way to new joint ventures, from collaborating with partners to using eco-friendly materials in architecture, design, and fashion, or engaging in projects that reduce the digital footprint in the audio-visual, video-game, or music industries (KEA & PPMI, 2019). The changing expectations of environmentally and socially alert generations are paving the path to new ways of brand communication. For example, peoples' interest in ethical and sustainable brands has grown during the pandemic (Brandwatch, 2020). Similar to other fields, the brands of cultural fields face the urgency of finding new ways to communicate to their audiences, "strengthening the brand with messages about durability, safety, professionalism, reliability, quality, trust, etc." (Krajnović et al., 2021) These messages have become the emphasis of brand communication. To secure brand loyalty in turbulent times, many cultural organisations applied the free-access strategy, similar to many magazines and journals. This is just one example of responding to the needs of customers that has developed in accordance with the ongoing "digital," "green," and "social responsibility" shifts.

In relation to business-model innovations, the sector is moving more and more towards intra- and cross-sectoral collaborations, which was listed as one of the effects of the COVID-19 crisis in the report by the European Parliament's Committee on Culture and Education (IDEA Consult et al., 2021). One of the ways to create added value to the core creative activities is collaboration with the research and development (R&D) sector. It is likely we will witness cultural organisations successfully collaborating with this innovative sector (Bakhshi et al., 2010) by creating more and more start-up companies. In cultural joint ventures focused on developing innovations that aim to solve social issues (KEA & PPMI, 2019), arts and cultural organisations might provide a great contribution. Even more, there is great potential for joint ventures to build a shared identity and a strong brand image once the barrier between R&D and cultural organisations is overcome. Partners from different industries that work together can both benefit from the integrated value arising from this collaboration (van der Pijl, 2018). Innovation exchanges across different cultural sectors and between research-based incubators, laboratories, universities, etc., are expected to increase and broaden (Gustafsson & Lazzaro, 2021).

The more these initiatives among the public, private, and nonprofit sectors become the new norm, a stronger ecosystem with specific competencies and abilities to support and sustain these joint ventures can develop. The more collaborative ventures are established between small and microenterprises, and between the public and business sectors, the greater are the chances that cultural joint ventures will emerge, grow, and flourish.

13.3 Changes in leadership and roles of members

In addition to changes in organisational forms, business models, and audiences, we foresee that the leadership and roles of engaged people in cultural joint ventures are changing. In light of recent trends, the probability of emergence of new ways of management and leadership is high. This means that the future leaders of cultural joint ventures will face new demands requiring different competencies and skills.

One of the future trends concerning organisational practices might be driven by the so-called disintermediation (see Draper, 2008). The tendency of "cutting out the middleman" greatly affects the structures and roles inside arts organisations. Along with the shortening of the value chain in the cultural and creative sector (especially with recorded music, see Kõlar, 2019), we can predict the elimination of some very specific roles in the arts sector, especially in the phases of creation and production. In return, this can open new opportunities and raise the need for attention to the distribution and consumption phases, in which branding will have a more substantial role than ever.

More importantly, disintermediation in the cultural and creative sector has led to changed dynamics and practices of art production, as the professional competencies of each participant involved are becoming more hybrid in nature. With the ability to produce, promote, and distribute quickly without intermediaries, the process empowers and yet, at the same time, fragments the focus of the artistic staff. The role of individual artists thus will become more crucial, as they will play a more important role in the production and distribution of cultural goods and services.

We see many initiatives in which the "face" has been given to individual musicians, orchestra members, and choirs through digital marketing channels. Artists share their personal stories, including the backstage and human side of the creative process. Therefore, the brands of art and cultural organisations are tending to become more human-centred, personalised, and relatable. Managing and leading the "stars" or pillars of the brands involves several distinct aspects that leaders should keep in mind. When the positions within organisational structures change such that there is a social media "influencer" instead of a marketing specialist, the leaders' functions are likely to modify. Leading from "behind the curtains" might require different competencies and the mindset of a "servant" leader. Curating rather than managing might be one of these scenarios. Engaging individual members who expect new networked ways of socialising and self-managing teams in all the steps from value creation to distribution and consumption forces leaders to practise new styles of leading in enabling higher levels of flexibility, autonomy, and multiple ways of connectivity (van der Pijl, 2018).

According to Dufva (2020a), members of the organisations want prospects, security, and opportunities for moving ahead, and the lack of these might cause frustration, withdrawal, and the adoption of extreme attitudes. From the perspective of cultural joint ventures, the forming of new communities based on differences in values and possible withdrawal might lead to unmanageable challenges. In this era of increased interconnectedness and interdependence, the personnel of joint ventures might even feel isolated and lonely together (Dufva, 2020a).

Managing relationships in the context of crises, pandemic or otherwise, in which people have less physical contact and more virtual collaboration, requires new competencies on the part of leaders. For instance, leaders' skills in building and maintaining communities becomes more important. In addition to venue-based activities in which the leader's main role is to support the engagement and forming of the joint identity, there is a need to give more attention to building and maintaining digital communities inside and outside of the organisation in the collaboration of joint ventures. It is not only about acquiring digital skills but also about developing communication, negotiation, and facilitation skills for the digital setting.

The development of new skillsets is reported to be a side effect of the COVID-19 pandemic (IDEA Consult et al., 2021). The emergence of new types of leaders is probably also more and more related to meeting the expectations of new generations and the work-life perceptions of employees of the Z and Alpha generations. At the same time, the understanding of and approach to the leadership of emerging generations is always grounded in the contexts, environmental conditions, and societal processes. Therefore, the skills that have served in the past for managing joint ventures can probably serve only partially in the future.

As noted in Part III, the identity and brand image of joint ventures relies on knowledge sharing, organisational structure, and a joint practice-oriented organisational culture. In the new era, the means and challenges of managing these aspects have somewhat changed and require special attention with new approaches. As we witnessed during the pandemic, in times of crisis, centralised decision-making tends to be more easily accepted during exceptional times, but after the acute crisis has receded, people find it even more important to continue the development of participatory democracy (Lähdemäki-Pekkonen & Ikäheimo, 2020). In turbulent times, leaders are required to make swift decisions and communicate about them in uncertain situations (Lähdemäki-Pekkonen & Ikäheimo, 2020). Therefore, there is a greater need for quick, knowledge-based decision-making without compromising democratic engagement. Therefore, we may see that more decision-making power is assigned to algorithms in the future (Dufva, 2020a).

The leaders of future joint ventures in the arts and culture sector will need to increase their knowledge of technology in order to make the best use of it and to embrace the digital shift and its opportunities. Their competence in managing consumption data also has to increase, as well as their ability to tackle the impacts of increased international market concentration, new consumption trends, and changing business paradigms (KEA, 2020). In addition, the ability to manage data use and data rights, to understand the impact of algorithms on behaviour, and to prepare for cybercrime (Dufva, 2020b) are part of the new demands for future leaders. In addition, the report by VVA (2021) points out that in the live performance and event sector, one of the crucial future skills needed will be the ability to build digital brands. The report points out the policy recommendations for sustainable skills in the cultural and creative industries sector and stresses the need for special attention to those skills that allow cross-sectoral collaboration (VVA 2021). As the recommendation hints at, there probably will be more boosting measures which support the emergence of joint ventures. At the same time, special capacity-building strategies (such as training programmes) will be supported and initiated in order to prepare the ground for more sustainable joint ventures.

In addition to the new demands for leaders' competencies in relation to technology developments, there are many possibilities for non-technological innovation (organisation, marketing, etc.), which demand different scales of skills and competencies. Organisations in the arts and cultural sector face the challenge of protecting their knowledge and innovation-based competitive advantages against new competitors from emergent countries (Plaza & Haarich, 2017). There is thus an increasing need to pay attention to competencies around non-technological innovations, including the protection of joint knowledge, identities, and brands. In the new reality, knowledge-sharing amidst the changing ways of working, including remote working, might be challenging, especially in the forming phase of new joint ventures.

Joint ventures where organisational structures, cultures, and practices come together and form a combined new one might lead to completely new solutions if the collaboration partners are no longer traditional organisations. The ability to build solid knowledge management and secure engagement when employees are largely working remotely requires either collaboration with specialised experts or special training and focus. When employees expect their organisation to consciously manage its societal impact, desire a greater sense of belonging, demand that more attention be paid to sustainability, ecology, and equality with new ways of behaviour, then the leaders' empathy, sensitivity, responsibility, and proactive attitudes become even more crucial.

In the post-pandemic new reality, the tendency to adopt quick changes, maintain the synergy under constant pressure, and face ongoing rapid changes definitely has an effect on organisational culture and leadership. In joint ventures, the recognition and proper preparation in relation to choosing the best partner match and compiling a "dream team" might become extremely important.

13.4 Conclusions

To conclude, there seems to be unused potential for business-model innovations, which motivates the forming of strong alliances and joint ventures more now than ever. Along with the trend of applying design thinking in managing cultural organisations, the trend of discovering alternative ways to create revenue streams and develop value propositions can be witnessed. The key partners across the sectors are leading the way in these innovative exchanges. Digitalisation and the rapid development of technological solutions are enabling more and more unforeseen solutions for cultural organisations in all the elements of business models, from core activities to distribution channels. There is also a clear need for new types of leadership in the new reality of joint ventures. The expected skillsets of the leaders range from traditional roles to managing new roles, technology, innovation, cross-sectorial tensions, and crises. The possible benefits of joining resources in joint ventures cannot be overstated in this process.

References

Bakhshi, H., Freeman, A., & Desai, R. (2010). *Not rocket science: A roadmap for arts and cultural R&D*. London: Mission Models Money. missionmodelsmoney.org.uk/sites/default/files/23974477-Not-Rocket-Science-Hasan-Bakhshi-et-al-2010_0.pdf

Baumol, W. J., & Bowen, W. G. (1966). *Performing arts, the economic dilemma: A study of problems common to theater, opera, music, and dance*. Cambridge, MA: MIT Press.

Betzler, D., Loots, E., Prokůpek, M., Marques, L., & Grafenauer, P. (2021). COVID-19 and the arts and cultural sectors: Investigating countries' contextual factors and early policy measures. *International Journal of Cultural Policy*, *27*(6), 796–814. https://doi.org/10.1080/10286632.2020.1842383

Brandwatch Research. (2020). *New research reveals how consumers view brand purpose in 2020*. www.brandwatch.com/reports/2020-brand-purpose/view

Buchoud, N. J. A., Eryuce, O., Gebetsberger, C., Newbigin, J., Avogadro, E., Damuri, Y. R., Frei-Oldenburg, A., Henderson, M., Khor, N., & Larasati, T. (2021). *Creative economy 2030: Inclusive and resilient creative economy for sustainable development and recovery policy brief. Task Force 5, 2030*. Agenda and Development Cooperation.

Compendium Cultural Policy & Trends. (2021, June). *Comparative overview: Reopening measures*. Retrieved March 20, 2022, from www.culturalpolicies.net/covid-19/comparative-overview-reopening/#1589291468699-c510eb9b-f5c6

Creative Clusters Ltd. (2022). *Key Concepts: Creative Clusters*. https://creativeclusters.com/?page_id=1599

Draper, P. (2008, November). On disintermediated culture, education, and craft. In *Fourth annual art of record production conference* (pp. 14–16). Lowell, MA. Griffith University, Queensland.

Dufva, M. (2020a). *The big picture of the megatrends SITRA*. www.sitra.fi/en/articles/the-big-picture-of-the-megatrends/

Dufva, M. (2020b), Technology is becoming embedded in everything. www.sitra.fi/en/articles/megatrend-4-technology-is-becoming-embedded-in-everything/

European Commission. (2021). *Advanced technologies for industry—Sectoral watch*. https://ati.ec.europa.eu/sites/default/files/2021-05/Sectoral%20Watch%20Creative%20Industry.pdf

Gustafsson, C., & Lazzaro, E. (2021). The innovative response of cultural and creative industries to major European societal challenges: Toward a knowledge and competence base. *Sustainability*, *13*, 13267. https://doi.org/10.3390/ su132313267

Hagoort, G. (2003). *Art management: Entrepreneurial style*. Eburon Uitgeverij BV.

IDEA Consult, Goethe-Institut, Amann, S., & Heinsius, J. (2021). *Research for CULT Committee—Cultural and creative sectors in post-Covid-19 Europe: Crisis effects and policy recommendations*. Brussels: European Parliament, Policy Department for Structural and Cohesion Policies.

KEA. (2020). *The impact of the COVID-19 pandemic on the cultural and creative sector*. Report for the Council of Europe. https://keanet.eu/wp-content/uploads/Impact-of-COVID-19-pandemic-on-CCS_COE-KEA_26062020.pdf

KEA & PPMI. (2019). *Research for CULT Committee—Culture and creative sectors in the European Union—Key future developments, challenges and opportunities*. Brussels: European Parliament, Policy Department for Structural and Cohesion Policies.

Khlystova, O., Kalyuzhnova, Y., & Belitski, M. (2022). The impact of the COVID-19 pandemic on the creative industries: A literature review and future research agenda. *Journal of Business Research*, *139*, 1192–1210.

Kõlar, J.-M. (2019). *Emerging patterns of digitalization in the Estonian music industry*. Estonian Business School. Tallinn, Estonia.

Krajnović, A., Vrdoljak, R. I., & Perković, A. (2021). Strategic and digital marketing in cultural institutions and the impact of the covid-19 pandemic—A comparative analysis of two case studies. *Interdisciplinary Description of Complex Systems: INDECS, 19*(2), 257–280.

Lähdemäki-Pekkonen, J., & Ikäheimo, H.-P. (2020).The coronavirus crisis is challenging participatory democracy. *SITRA*. www.sitra.fi/en/articles/the-coronavirus-crisis-is-challenging-participatory-democracy/

Organisation for Economic Co-operation and Development (OECD). (2020). *Culture shock: COVID-19 and the cultural and creative sectors*. OECD Publishing. Paris, France. https://read.oecd-ilibrary.org/view/?ref=135_135961-nenh9f2w7a&title=Culture-shock-COVID-19-and-the-cultural-and-creative-sectors

Plaza, B., & Haarich, S. N. (2017). Arts, culture and creativity as drivers for territorial development, innovation and competitiveness. In V. Ateca-Amestoy, V. Ginsburgh, I. Mazza, J. O'Hagan, & J. Prieto-Rodriguez (Eds.), *Enhancing participation in the arts in the EU*. Cham: Springer.

Ruusuvirta, M. (2019). Does sector matter? Plural characteristics and logics in third sector festival organisations. *JYU Dissertations, 60*. Jyväskylä, Finland.

UNESCO. (2021). *Cultural and creative industries in the face of COVID-19: An economic impact outlook*. https://en.unesco.org/creativity/publications/cultural-creative-industries-face-covid-19

van der Pijl, P. (2018). *How to design exponential (10x) business models?* Business Models Inc. San Francisco, USA. https://businessmodelsinc.medium.com/how-to-design-exponential-10x-business-models-decfc99e482b

VVA. (2021). *Creative FLIP final report, work package 2 on learning*. Goethe-Institut on behalf of Creative FLIP Project. Brussels.

Part V

Final words

This part highlights the key findings and conclusions related to the identity-image view on managing cultural joint ventures. It includes examples from the case studies and suggestions for future research. The book closes by presenting a model or framework of the key aspects of managing multiple identities and brands in the context of cultural joint ventures.

DOI: 10.4324/9780429273919-18

14 Concluding on the key points

In the previous parts, we elaborated on the identity and branding of cultural joint ventures. The focus of cultural joint ventures seems at times to be rather like any joint venture irrespective of the field, and the scholarly work from a wide array of fields and industries has been used to reveal the key elements and dimensions under study. Yet, at the same time, the specificities of culture and art are highlighted, as they have an effect on the ways the identity and brand image are created, managed, and received by managers and customers. In the next summary, the specifics of art and culture are reflected upon in terms of each of the elements of our proposed managerial model for cultural joint ventures, building on the insights from the discussions and elaborations on the research considered in the previous parts.

Through our research path, some challenges and fears manifested in relation to joint ventures, especially in the cultural field, and also to the nature of cultural organisations as such. In a setting in which partners retain their distinct identities but hold a vision of joint community identity, ambiguities and confusion regarding identity and image may exist. The complex network of identities and image formation among the collaborative actors can thus present real challenges in managing cultural joint ventures. Next, we tackle these fears and reflect on the insights gained as possible avenues for solutions.

In Part I, we focused on organisational identity and recognised that cross- and inter-organisational identity building occurs and is co-created through a network of identities occurring at different levels—individual, team, organisation, and joint-venture. We identified that the joining elements of the plethora of identities represent the core value and the core activities around that value, which is making art. In the case of the Helsinki Music Centre, even before the actualisation of the joint venture, the different actors shared similar visions and fears about the future. The orchestras and the music academy dreamt about a music house that would be an active venue full of people and music and feared an empty chapel for classical music that would be closed to people.

DOI: 10.4324/9780429273919-19

Another fear was that the Helsinki Music Centre would be taken over by entirely nonmusical activities, such as conferences. Similar fears or tensions were identified in the other cases as well. For example, in Harpa in Reykjavík, the music ensembles were given priority to use the spaces, yet Harpa's current image seems also to build strongly from architectural appreciation as well as touristic offerings. On the other hand, attracting tourists to admire the building, or offering touristic shows on nature might create interest towards Harpa's musical offerings as well. The shared vision and the underlying value, which is the love of art or music, seem to enable joint identity-building for cultural joint ventures, providing a base for a community unified by these expressions.

The role of the core value and how it manifests itself in identity at different levels of organisations and joint ventures needs further research. It would be especially interesting to discover its role at the individual and team levels of cultural organisations and joint ventures and to elaborate on how these levels play a role in building the joint-venture identity.

When looking at the joint-venture identity and the core value, the love of art, from a brand-image perspective, we want to emphasise that the brand image is always connected to the organisational identity. While the internal identity aims to build a joint base for joint activities and cross-fertilisation between the key actors and music genres inside the organisation or organisations in the joint venture, the external identity aims to capture and relate to the existing and potential audiences. In the case of the Helsinki Music Centre, the key actors, HBO, RSO, and the Sibelius Academy all seemed to have strong, loyal customer groups as their audience, and the Helsinki Music Centre is seen as the venue: a place filled with music in which to meet and interact.

This led us to propose that the brand image of the Helsinki Music Centre, the joint venture, is endorsed by the sub-brands that actually create the content and meaning for their own brands, and the Helsinki Music Centre as a cultural joint venture is the place to experience these meanings and content. On the other hand, in the case of Concertgebaum in Amsterdam, the original brand of the venues and its main actors are related to the content, and build the main brand image for this joint venture. The other actors are endorsed by the brand of Concertgebaum, irrespective of being regular visiting organisations or more permanent organisations hosted by Concertgebaum.

Our findings point out that those organisations in which the umbrella brand, i.e., the hosting organisation, has artistic productions of its own, the brand identity was strongly linked to the hosting organisation's brand identity, whereas in situations where the hosting umbrella organisation was mainly responsible for the space management and marketing, the sub-brands' organisational identities had a major role. Thus, joint artistic activities usually lead to the brand strategies of sub-brands or branded house strategies, whereas in cases in which only space/marketing activities are shared, the brand architecture strategy is the house of brands or endorsing sub-brands strategy. These findings provide us with interesting reflections on identity- and brand-building and on the role of internal and external activities, which may change our ways of engaging in the brand-building processes. Thus, we highlight the role of joint content activities and propose this as an interesting avenue for future research.

The identified brand architecture strategies are only one way to manage and join brands. The different approaches discussed in Part II, such as brand extensions, co-branding, and brand alliances, provide managers with other tools and ways to understand and build branding, for organisations and joint ventures alike. The multiple examples found in the art and cultural fields indicate that these tools are usable and relevant for the arts sector as well. However, due to the specific nature of this field, we emphasise that adopting any of the managerial branding tools needs careful reflection on the nature of the art and how the branding tool can be adapted to address the artistic values within the field. Thus, even though branding in art organisations seems to be accepted as a managerial activity aimed at building organisational identities and profiles—both internally and from the perspectives of stakeholders—especially with regards to audiences, and it is also used in joint ventures, we encourage critical reflection on the branding which acknowledges the core value of the love of art and its implications, rather than using branding merely as a technical tool.

As the case examples in Part II point out, branding can also be used on an individual level, as artists' names and the specificities of their art have been considered as brands. Yet, artists have also used branding as a trigger for creating art, providing novel perspectives and criticism of brands and branding phenomena. Indeed, the relationship between art and branding is an interesting societal phenomenon to explore in further research. In addition, the changing roles of customers and audiences, as well as the new ways of consumption, impact the ways brands are experienced and how customers attach meaning to them. Especially in organisations with traditionally strong and loyal customers, these new trends require deeper understanding and research on how they affect cultural joint ventures that traditionally build on such customer bases.

Part III elaborated on how organisational structure, culture, and practices affect the joint venture and the key issues to acknowledge when joining cultural organisations in joint ventures, in which two existing organisational structures, cultures, and practices are combined. As discussed above, the role of the core value and the sharing of content activities—in the case of art, artistic activities—are vital, as they enable the sharing of knowledge, joint learning, and the building of a joint identity and brand image. The role of supporting activities, such as venue management and marketing, can, however, play a role in triggering the visioning and motivation for joint identity, building from the case example of the Helsinki Music Centre. However, if these activities are only shared without the joint visioning and sharing of content, the identities most likely remain separate, as shown in the case of Auckland Live in New Zealand.

In addition to the key role of the core value and the sharing of content activities, the national identity and the role of the parent organisation were found to affect the identity and brand image-building processes in joint ventures. This has also been discovered in research on joint ventures within other industries and contexts; hence, it cannot be seen as a unique feature for cultural joint ventures (see more in Part III). The national identity as well as the parent organisation's identity affect the organisational culture and thus need to be recognised when building a joint venture. Even if their effect is known, there is a need for further research on their role, especially when considering the future forms of joint ventures, such as hybrid or virtual and global or local, as discussed in Part IV. In addition, special attention should be paid to the emergence of joint ventures of art and cultural organisations with organisations from other fields that do not share a similar core value, i.e., the love of art. How is it possible to build a joint identity when there is no evident original core value to be shared?

To conclude, we return to the key elements of the identity-image. On the one hand, it is about building commonalities with respect to organisations, individuals, and cross-organisations, while at the same time creating differences, or ways to distinguish one's own identity and image from others—in other words, creating boundaries. We need to keep in mind that boundaries act in two ways: they create the community by distinguishing it from other communities, and they differentiate and build borders between the communities. In addition, boundaries can inhibit a new community from emerging, or a new joint identity in the case of joint ventures, as the boundaries of existing communities and organisations can impede the construction of new ones.

Similar to identity, the boundaries exist on various levels, and they can relate simultaneously to a network of communities and identities rather than just a single identity. Hence, in creating a joint venture, the boundaries need to be dismantled on the one hand to enable the building of the new entity and on the other hand to create new joint boundaries for the new joint identity and image. The boundaries are built through organisational culture and structure and can be recreated through practice: consciously developing joint shared practice, especially focusing on the key content and basing the practice on shared core values. The new hybrid forms of joint ventures, the global context, and digitalisation create new challenges for boundary work, which are topics for further research.

15 Towards a model of identity-image management of cultural joint ventures

As discussed above, cultural joint ventures have at the core of their identity and image the valuation of art, which is the key element in their identity-image. The structure in art organisations has been traditionally described as hierarchical, on the one hand building on expertise and stardom, and on the other hand on teamwork. It has been proposed that in art organisations, "the closer you are to the stage, or artistic creation, the more important and valued you are," whereas the supporting services, even if based on specific expertise, are viewed as less valuable. However, recent changes might indicate a move towards less hierarchical organisational structures and cultures, as the expertise of costume designers, stage managers, etc., are also presented, acknowledged, and connected to the organisation's identity and image in social media, for example. In addition, the recent challenges have forced organisations to adopt flexible, responsive management styles that are hard to maintain in a hierarchical organisational culture with non-flexible structures (see more in Part IV).

The following figure illustrates a more flexible organisational model for cultural joint ventures, with an emphasis on core values and the sharing of content practices, as well as the integration of the identity-image connectivity, acknowledging the role of audiences, customers, and stakeholders in cultural joint ventures' identity-image management and (co-)creation.

First, the traditional hierarchical organisational structure of many cultural organisations does not allow for the rapid adaptability required by managers today to respond and collaborate when facing unexpected challenges in society, or in relation to the changing needs and perceptions of customers. In joint ventures, building shared ways to adapt and respond adds more resources and competencies to counter the risks and changes they face from the external environment.

Second, the organisational culture reflects the organisational structures, and an emphasis on building teams and a sense of community allows for the recognition of a wider variety of talent and expertise within cultural

DOI: 10.4324/9780429273919-20

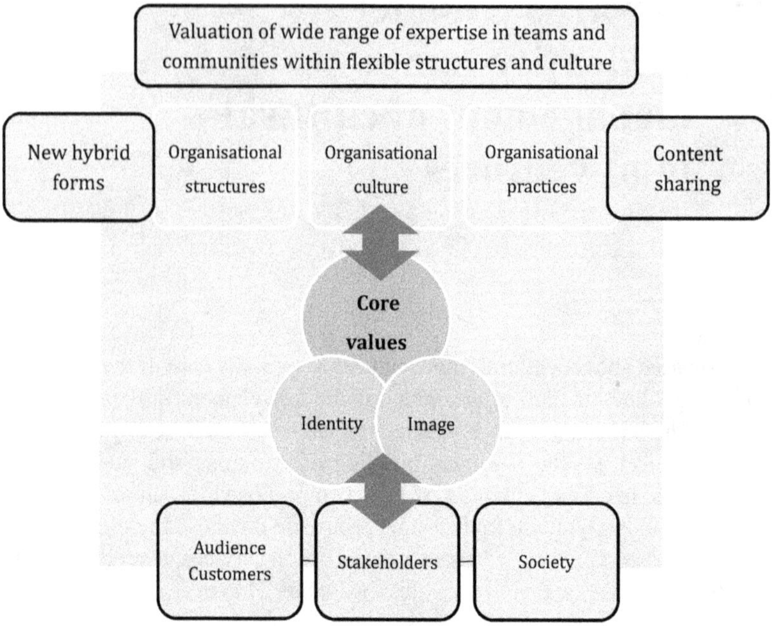

Figure 15.1 The key elements of cultural joint ventures

organisations, without losing the respect for the core value, which is art. However, the emphasis on communities inherently presents the danger of borders, as discussed earlier; therefore, the management needs to create cross-community and cross-organisational practices, as well as practices that relate to the organisation's core content, in direct or indirect ways. In joint ventures, recognising that the intertwined communities are based, for example, on professions, and also on key content practices to be shared, would be a good starting point to build cross-organisational practices. On the other hand, the new hybrid formal joint ventures with organisations outside the arts and cultural field needs more explicit work in order to identify the common core value(s) and content that enable the building of a joint identity.

Third, identity and image are intertwined and influence each other. How we see our organisation, community, or cross-organisation influences their identity and how the messages and interpretations of the image are created and built from the identity. However, not only the formal message through, for example, marketing and social media forms the image, but also the interpretations of identity the employees implicitly or explicitly share inside and outside the organisation contribute to creating the image. In joint ventures, understanding the organisational identity with its multiple levels and core values enables us to proceed with building the joint identity and creating an image that acknowledges the organisation as whole, and which is based on the shared value, or the discovered one.

Last, it is important to acknowledge that the organisational identity and image not only emerge from the inside, but also the audiences/customers and other stakeholders co-create both identity and image. Many customers share the same core values and expect to see these manifested in an organisation's activities, as well as its messages, which build the image of the organisation. Likewise, societal values and changes affect individual values and what is perceived as right or wrong, and, as such, influence the individual identities as well as the organisational values and identity. Similarly, joint ventures need to acknowledge the changing values and changing customers, and the potential differences in these, when planning a joint practice and co-creating a shared identity and image.

To conclude, we wish to emphasise that the conceptualisation of joint ventures, including the various forms and ways in which joint ventures may take place in the future, is enlarging. We thus strongly recommend further study on the new elaborations and understandings of joint ventures, in the cultural sector and in other sectors.

Index